LSAT®

PrepTest 86

Unlocked

Deconstructing the November 2018 LSAT

© 2019 by Kaplan, Inc.

Published by Kaplan Publishing, a division of Kaplan, Inc.
750 Third Avenue
New York, NY 10017

ISBN: 978-1-5062-4981-0
10 9 8 7 6 5 4 3 2 1

Table of Contents

The Inside Story 1

Section I: Logical Reasoning 7

Section II: Logic Games 19

Section III: Reading Comprehension 29

Section IV: Logical Reasoning 46

Glossary 59

The Inside Story

PrepTest 86 was administered in November 2018. What made this test so hard? Here's a breakdown of what Kaplan students who were surveyed after taking the official exam considered PrepTest 86's most difficult section.

Hardest PrepTest 86 Section as Reported by Test Takers

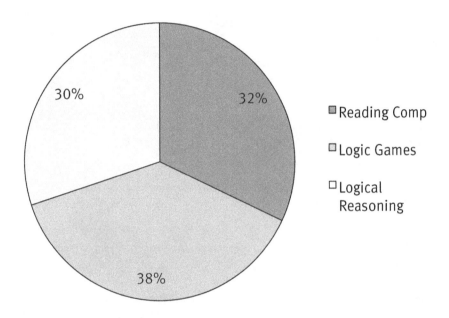

Based on these results, you might think that studying Logic Games is the key to LSAT success. Well, Logic Games is important, but test takers' perceptions don't tell the whole story. For that, you need to consider students' actual performance. The following chart shows the average number of students to miss each question in each of PrepTest 86's different sections.

Percentage Incorrect by PrepTest 86 Section Type

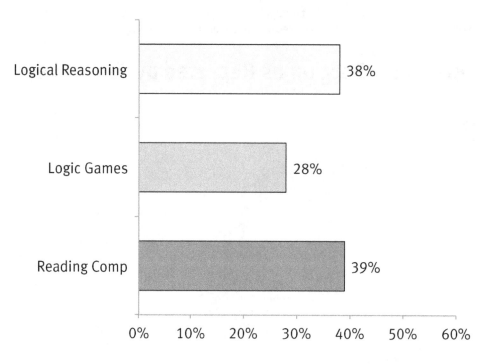

Actual student performance tells quite a different story. On average, students were actually more likely to miss questions in Logical Reasoning and Reading Comprehension—by a fairly wide margin—than they were in Logic Games.

Maybe students overestimate the difficulty of the Logic Games section because it's so unusual, or maybe it's because a really hard Logic Game is so easy to remember after the test. But the truth is that the testmaker places hard questions throughout the test. Here were the locations of the 10 hardest (most missed) questions in the exam.

Location of the 10 Most Difficult Questions in PrepTest 86

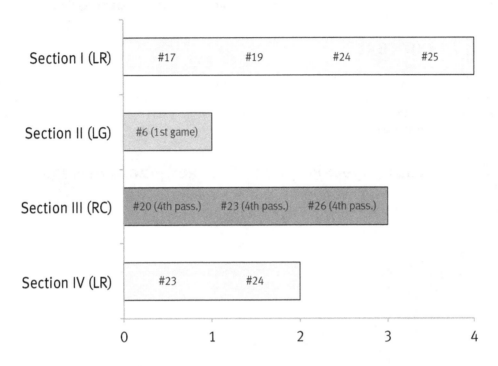

The takeaway from this data is that, to maximize your potential on the LSAT, you need to take a comprehensive approach. Test yourself rigorously, and review your performance on every section of the test. Kaplan's LSAT explanations provide the expertise and insight you need to fully understand your results. The explanations are written and edited by a team of LSAT experts, who have helped thousands of students improve their scores. Kaplan always provides data-driven analysis of the test, ranking the difficulty of every question based on actual student performance. The 10 hardest questions on every test are highlighted with a 4-star difficulty rating, the highest we give. The analysis breaks down the remaining questions into 1-, 2-, and 3-star ratings so that you can compare your performance to thousands of other test takers on all LSAC material.

Don't settle for wondering whether a question was really as hard as it seemed to you. Analyze the test with real data, and learn the secrets and strategies that help top scorers master the LSAT.

7 Can't-Miss Features of PrepTest 86

- 99 questions! This was the first test ever to have less than 100 questions. It was also the first test to have 26—instead of 27—Reading Comprehension questions since December 2006 (PT 51).
- PrepTest 86 is an excellent test for seeing a variety of question types in Logical Reasoning. Over the previous three years some question types like Main Point, Method of Argument, Point at Issue, and Role of Statement were entirely missing from a single test. However, on PrepTest 86 there were two of each of them.
- Crazy eights! PrepTest 86 featured an even mix of the major Assumption Family questions with eight each of Assumption, Flaw, and Strengthen/Weaken. This was the first test to do so since PrepTest June 2007.
- A trend continues! The Logic Games section has only started with a Hybrid game 10 times ever. That said, PrepTest 86 was the fifth test in the last eight released tests to do so!
- It may start with a Hybrid game, but it's all Strict Sequencing after that. That makes this the seventh test to feature three Strict Sequencing games, and the first since June 2013 (PT 69).
- That last RC passage is a doozy! With three 4-Star questions and no 1-Star questions, it is one of only six passages ever where the average question difficulty is over three stars.

- Ariana Grande's "Thank U, Next" sat atop the billboard charts the week PrepTest 86 was administered. Even though the lyrics are clearly not about test-taking, the message about learning from each relationship and moving on is good advice for LSAT practice. Each PrepTest is an opportunity to learn a bit more and be better prepared for the next one.

PrepTest 86 in Context

As much fun as it is to find out what makes a PrepTest unique or noteworthy, it's even more important to know just how representative it is of other LSAT administrations (and, thus, how likely it is to be representative of the exam you will face on Test Day). The following charts compare the numbers of each kind of question and game on PrepTest 86 to the average numbers seen on all officially released LSATs administered over the past five years (from 2014 through 2018).

Number of LR Questions by Type: PrepTest 86 vs. 2014–2018 Average

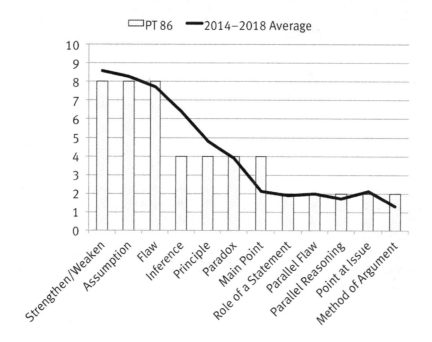

Number of LG Games by Type: PrepTest 86 vs. 2014–2018 Average

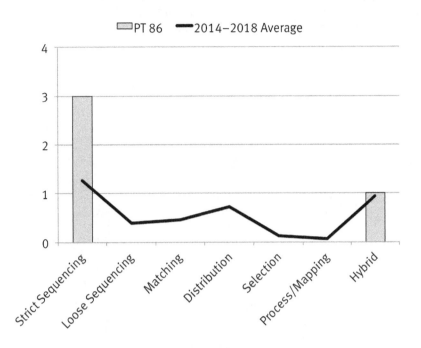

Number of RC Questions by Type: PrepTest 86 vs. 2014–2018 Average

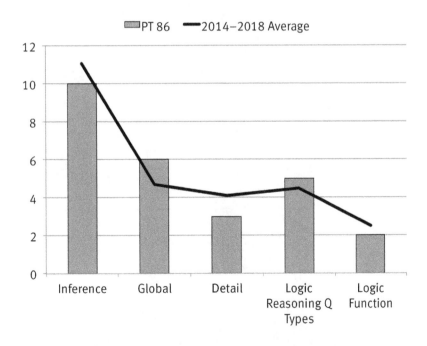

There isn't usually a huge difference in the distribution of questions from LSAT to LSAT, but if this test seems harder (or easier) to you than another you've taken, compare the number of questions of the types on which you, personally, are strongest and weakest. And then, explore within each section to see if your best or worst question types came earlier or later.

Students in Kaplan's comprehensive LSAT courses have access to every released LSAT and to a library of thousands of officially released questions arranged by question, game, and passage type. If you are studying on your own, you have to do a bit more work to identify your strengths and your areas of opportunity. Quantitative analysis (like that in the charts shown here) is an important tool for understanding how the test is constructed, and how you are performing on it.

Section I: Logical Reasoning

Q#	Question Type	Correct	Difficulty
1	Strengthen	E	★
2	Main Point	D	★
3	Weaken	B	★
4	Main Point	A	★
5	Assumption (Necessary)	A	★
6	Paradox (EXCEPT)	D	★
7	Assumption (Sufficient)	C	★
8	Flaw	D	★
9	Principle (Identify/Strengthen)	C	★
10	Inference	E	★
11	Principle (Identify/Strengthen)	C	★
12	Assumption (Sufficient)	B	★★
13	Paradox	C	★★
14	Weaken	B	★★★
15	Flaw	A	★★
16	Assumption (Necessary)	B	★★★
17	Point At Issue (Agree)	E	★★★★
18	Paradox	B	★★
19	Flaw	D	★★★★
20	Principle (Identify/Strengthen)	B	★★★
21	Flaw	B	★★★
22	Inference	D	★★
23	Parallel Reasoning	D	★★★
24	Method of Argument	E	★★★★
25	Parallel Flaw	A	★★★★

1. (E) Strengthen

Step 1: Identify the Question Type
The question asks for something that "strengthens the [given] argument," making this a Strengthen question.

Step 2: Untangle the Stimulus
The researcher mentions that bonobos eat certain leaves during the rainy season. The researcher then concludes that they eat the leaves for a medicinal purpose. The evidence (*since*) is that eating the leaves helps eliminate gastrointestinal worms.

Step 3: Make a Prediction
While getting rid of gastrointestinal worms would certainly be a medicinal benefit, there's no evidence that bonobos have those worms or are eating the leaves for that purpose. Maybe bonobos just like the taste of those leaves. The author assumes otherwise, and the correct answer should make it more likely that bonobos are indeed eating the leaves for health reasons.

Step 4: Evaluate the Answer Choices
(E) is correct. This confirms that, when the bonobos eat the leaves (the rainy season), the bonobos have the worms. That makes it more likely that they are eating the leaves to help eliminate those worms.

(A) is Out of Scope. Even if bonobos only eat the leaves of *M. fulvum*, that doesn't mean it's for medicinal purposes. They may just like the taste.

(B) is Out of Scope. Even if other animals eat the same or similar leaves, there's still no evidence that any of them are eating the leaves for medicinal purposes. Again, the leaves just might be tasty.

(C) is a 180, at worst. This just suggests that bonobos are eating these leaves because they're readily available. They may not care about the medicinal benefit. They just care about the easy pickings.

(D) is a Distortion. This may help explain why bonobos eat these leaves during the rainy season. However, it does nothing to confirm that the leaves are eaten for medicinal purposes.

2. (D) Main Point

Step 1: Identify the Question Type
The question asks for the "overall conclusion" of the argument, making this a Main Point question.

Step 2: Untangle the Stimulus
The analyst starts out with the opinion of other people—those concerned with safeguarding public health. However, this question is about the analyst's conclusion, not other people's conclusion. The Contrast Keyword [*b*]*ut* indicates the analyst's rebuttal of the other people's conclusion: Reducing travel mileage would actually be the best automotive-related way to safeguard public health. The last sentence is directly presented as a *fact*, which means it's evidence to support the author's conclusion.

Step 3: Make a Prediction
The main conclusion is the analyst's rebuttal: Reducing travel mileage would be a better way to safeguard public health than other automotive safety measures.

Step 4: Evaluate the Answer Choices
(D) matches the analyst's conclusion.

(A) is a Faulty Use of Detail. This is the opinion of other people, not the analyst. And while the analyst might agree that reducing fatalities could help, that's not analyst's point. The analyst argues that reducing travel mileage is an even *better* solution.

(B) is a 180. The analyst suggests that a better plan would be to focus on reducing travel mileage.

(C) is a Faulty Use of Detail. This is the evidence used by the other people to support their point of view. While the analyst might agree that these measures would help, it misses the analyst's point that there's a better solution: focus on reducing travel mileage.

(E) is a Faulty Use of Detail. This is directly presented as a fact in the last sentence, and thus serves as evidence to support the analyst's conclusion. It's not the conclusion itself.

3. (B) Weaken

Step 1: Identify the Question Type
The question asks for something that "weakens the argument," making this a Weaken question.

Step 2: Untangle the Stimulus
The letter writer concludes that a certain newspaper is biased toward movies over live theater. The evidence is that the paper has published five times as many movie reviews as it has live theater reviews.

Step 3: Make a Prediction
The letter writer is making the unwarranted assumption that more reviews is somehow indicative of a bias. There may be plenty of other reasons why the paper publishes more movie reviews: Maybe readers demand more movie reviews. Maybe the paper receives more financial incentives to write movie reviews. Maybe there are just a lot more movies to review. To weaken the argument, a correct answer can point to one of these or any other alternative explanation.

Step 4: Evaluate the Answer Choices
(B) is correct. If there are a lot more movies, then publishing more movie reviews is not a sign of bias. It's a sign of what the paper has available for reviewing.

(A) is Out of Scope. Even if other papers are publishing no live theater reviews, that doesn't mean the paper in question is any less biased for having a scant number of reviews. It's still printing five times as many movie reviews.

(C) is a 180. This, if anything, could help confirm the paper's bias. If it was really unbiased, it would be more reasonable to have an equal number of movie and live theater critics.

(D) is a Distortion. Even if the paper doesn't have the space to print reviews of everything, this still doesn't offer a plausible reason why the paper prints far more movie reviews. Why aren't the numbers more equal? The author could still claim a bias.

(E) is an Irrelevant Comparison. Even if the paper increased its live theater reviews from one year to the next, movie reviews were still five times more common. There could still be a bias.

4. (A) Main Point

Step 1: Identify the Question Type
The question asks for the "overall conclusion," making this a Main Point question.

Step 2: Untangle the Stimulus
The archaeologist begins with a fact: The university museum has some artifacts. The archaeologist then presents a general principle: Important artifacts belong to the nation in which they were discovered. Based on that principle, the archaeologist makes a recommendation: The museum should return the artifacts.

Step 3: Make a Prediction
Recommendations are often conclusions, and that's certainly the case here. The conclusion is that the artifacts should be returned, with the principle and the given facts providing support for that conclusion.

Step 4: Evaluate the Answer Choices
(A) is correct.

(B) is a Faulty Use of Detail. This is the principle in the second sentence, which the archaeologist uses as support for the conclusion. It's not itself the conclusion.

(C) is a Faulty Use of Detail. This is a given fact at the beginning of the second sentence. However, despite that fact, the archaeologist still argues that the artifacts should be returned. That's the conclusion.

(D) is a Faulty Use of Detail. This is just a fact provided in the first sentence. The conclusion is that the museum should return these artifacts.

(E) is a Faulty Use of Detail. The archaeologist acknowledges such a principle, but that just provides a basis for the actual conclusion. Because of that principle, the archaeologist argues that the museum's artifacts should be returned.

5. (A) Assumption (Necessary)

Step 1: Identify the Question Type
The question asks for an "assumption on which the argument depends," making this a Necessary Assumption question.

Step 2: Untangle the Stimulus
The author concludes ([*thus*]) that the supposedly precognitive characters in some works of fiction are not truly precognitive. The evidence is that these characters sometimes predict events that don't happen, which makes the predictions inaccurate.

Step 3: Make a Prediction
The author only claims that *some* of the predictions don't happen. However, what about all of the predictions that *do* happen? Couldn't the characters still be precognitive even if they get a couple of things wrong? The author argues otherwise, assuming that truly precognitive characters would *always* be right.

Step 4: Evaluate the Answer Choices
(A) matches the prediction, and is correct.

(B) is Extreme. The author doesn't have to believe that true precognition is *impossible*. Even if it is possible, the author is merely arguing that the fictional characters don't have the ability.

(C) is Out of Scope. Even if there are books that don't reveal whether or not the predicted event happens, the author's argument is about those books in which it *is* revealed that the events don't happen.

(D) is Out of Scope. It doesn't matter whether the supposed precognition is important or of little consequence to the story. The argument is solely about whether or not it can be truly considered precognition.

(E) is Extreme. The author only states that works of fiction *often* show that the characters are not truly precognitive. That doesn't mean it *never* happens.

6. (D) Paradox (EXCEPT)

Step 1: Identify the Question Type
The question is asking for information that "helps to explain" something surprising, which indicates a Paradox question. The EXCEPT indicates that the four wrong choices will resolve the paradox. The correct answer will not, either having no effect or making the result even more inexplicable.

Step 2: Untangle the Stimulus
The author mentions that worldwide employment is down. As would be expected, with fewer people working, there are fewer workplace injuries. However, the surprising result is that the *rate* of injuries is now lower.

Step 3: Make a Prediction

The numeric decreases make sense. If a company has a certain injury rate (say, 5%), then fewer employees would mean fewer injuries. (For example, with a 5% injury rate, 50 people would get injured in a company of 1,000 people, but only 5 people would get injured in a company of 100 people.) However, the mystery here is not about the numbers decreasing but about the injury rate decreasing. That suggests that workplaces are getting safer. Why would that be? There are countless potential reasons. Four choices will explain how workplaces are getting safer. The correct answer will be irrelevant or make it harder to explain.

Step 4: Evaluate the Answer Choices

(D) is correct. This just makes the mystery even harder to understand. If companies have fewer resources devoted to workplace safety, then injury rates should be getting worse. There's still no explanation how they're getting better.

(A) helps explain the result. If people are spending less time at work, then there's less time for injuries to happen.

(B) helps explain the result. If workers are less pressured, they're less likely to be hasty and commit injury-inducing behavior.

(C) helps explain the result. If the most dangerous jobs are losing a lot of people, then it's more likely that people are keeping safer jobs that would produce fewer injuries.

(E) helps explain the result. Inexperienced workers are likely more prone to injury, so getting rid of a greater number of inexperienced workers would probably help reduce the injury rate.

7. (C) Assumption (Sufficient)

Step 1: Identify the Question Type

The question asks for an assumption, one that would "allow the conclusion to be properly drawn." In other words, the assumption has to be good enough to guarantee the conclusion, making this a Sufficient Assumption question.

Step 2: Untangle the Stimulus

The editorial provides a ground rule for animated films. To be appropriate for children, they need to be whimsical, but they cannot be threatening. The editorial then mentions how some new animated films have dark themes. The conclusion from that is that these films are not appropriate for children.

Step 3: Make a Prediction

By the definition in the first sentence, a film would be inappropriate if it lacked whimsy or if it was threatening. However, it's only said that these new films have dark themes. The editorial assumes that those dark themes either lack whimsy or are threatening. Either of those assumptions would ensure that the films are inappropriate, as the editorial concludes.

Step 4: Evaluate the Answer Choices

(C) is correct. If the dark themes are threatening, then that guarantees the films are inappropriate for children, based on the logic of the first sentence.

(A) is a Distortion. Even if whimsical and threatening were mutually exclusive, there's still no evidence that the movies with dark themes fail to meet the standards for appropriateness.

(B) is not good enough. Even if films for adults are *seldom* appropriate for children, the new animated films could be an exception.

(D) is Out of Scope. The argument is not about whether children enjoy the film. It's about whether or not the film is appropriate.

(E) is Out of Scope. Whether or not kids are paying attention to the dark themes, there's still no evidence whether such themes are inappropriate.

8. (D) Flaw

Step 1: Identify the Question Type

The question asks why the "argument is flawed," making this a Flaw question. In addition, the question stem already identifies the flaw as an overlooked possibility, so be sure to consider alternative explanations.

Step 2: Untangle the Stimulus

According to the author, there are parasites that can affect the ability of monarch butterflies to fly. The author concludes ("[t]his shows") that migrating helps the butterflies avoid those parasites. The evidence is that only 15% of migrating butterflies have the parasites while a whopping 95% of non-migrating butterflies have the parasites.

Step 3: Make a Prediction

The author is making a causal argument, suggesting that the act of migration is what causes the migrating butterflies to avoid the parasites. However, it's likely that the author has the logic backwards. After all, the parasites are said to interfere with flying. Perhaps the migrating butterflies were mostly parasite-free to begin with, and the non-migrating butterflies aren't migrating because they've already been affected by the parasites. The author overlooks that possibility, and the correct answer should point that out.

Step 4: Evaluate the Answer Choices

(D) is correct. It's not that migrating affects the number of parasites a butterfly has, as the author suggests. It's the other way around, as this choice suggests: Parasites affect whether or not the butterfly migrates.

(A) is Out of Scope. Even if the butterflies can't detect the parasites, the author could still have a point about migrating helping the butterflies out.

(B) is an Irrelevant Comparison. The author is not claiming that longer migration is better. If even a short migration is enough to avoid parasites, then longer migrations don't need to be any better.

(C) is an Irrelevant Comparison. The argument is about the likelihood (or percentage) of getting parasites. The actual size of the groups (or number of butterflies) doesn't matter.

(E) is Out of Scope. It doesn't matter why a butterfly would choose to migrate or not. The argument is solely about whether migration would help the butterflies.

9. (C) Principle (Identify/Strengthen)

Step 1: Identify the Question Type
The question asks for a principle that "most justifies" something, making this an Identify the Principle question that acts like a Strengthen question. The stimulus has an unusual format. It provides a legal doctrine and a supposed application. If the application needs to be justified, it must be missing some important component of the given doctrine. Look for what's missing, and the correct answer should be a general rule that provides the missing piece.

Step 2: Untangle the Stimulus
The doctrine claims that the government has to offer fair compensation when it appropriates someone's private property. In trying to apply this doctrine, the author claims that the government has to offer fair compensation if it wants to block construction on certain private property, thus diminishing the property's market value.

Step 3: Make a Prediction
The doctrine requires fair compensation for *appropriation*. However, the application never mentions whether the situation described (blocking construction and diminishing market value) constitutes appropriation. In order to properly apply the doctrine and demand fair compensation, the correct answer must tie blocking construction or diminishing market value to the concept of appropriation.

Step 4: Evaluate the Answer Choices
(C) is correct. This characterizes the government's action in the application as appropriation, which confirms that the doctrine applies.

(A) is an Irrelevant Comparison. The doctrine is not about applying regulations consistently from one type of property to another. And this does nothing to confirm that the application fits the concept of appropriation.

(B) is Out of Scope. There is nothing in the doctrine or the application about wilderness.

(D) is Out of Scope. There is nothing in the doctrine or the application about economic risks.

(E) is Out of Scope. There is nothing in the doctrine or the application about public interest.

10. (E) Inference

Step 1: Identify the Question Type
The correct answer will fill in the blank at the end of the stimulus. That blank is the end of a sentence beginning with the Conclusion Keyword [*s*]*o*. That means the last sentence will be supported by the information before it, making this an Inference question.

Step 2: Untangle the Stimulus
According to the stimulus, a bird's shoulder joints are exposed to tremendous forces when flying. In order to fly, the bird must have stable wings, which means those forces have to be balanced. And balancing those forces can only be done with a certain ligament that connects the wing to the shoulder joint.

Step 3: Make a Prediction
The stimulus is basically one long string of Formal Logic. To fly, birds need stable wings, which in turn requires balancing forces, which in turn requires the ligament described.

$$\text{If} \quad \text{fly} \quad \rightarrow \quad \begin{array}{c}\textit{stable} \\ \textit{wings}\end{array} \quad \rightarrow \quad \begin{array}{c}\textit{balance} \\ \textit{forces}\end{array} \quad \rightarrow \quad \textit{ligament}$$

The last statement is a deduction about the ligament. The logic shows that the ligament is needed not only for balancing forces, but also for providing the stable wings needed for flight. The correct answer will likely follow the logic and describe this additional role the ligament plays.

Step 4: Evaluate the Answer Choices
(E) is correct, as the logic implies that the ligament is required for stabilizing the wings.

(A) is Extreme. While the ligament is certainly indispensable, it cannot be said to be the *only* indispensable structure. There could be many other structures that are needed for flight.

(B) gets the logic backwards. The ligament is not the reason why the wings need to be stable. The need for stable wings is the reason why the bird needs the ligament. There's no indication why the wings need to be stable.

(C) is Out of Scope. The ligament is the only connection mentioned, as it's required for balancing forces. However, there could be any number of unmentioned structures that connect the wing to the shoulder joint.

(D) is a Distortion. The ligament helps balance those forces. It is not the source of those forces.

11. (C) Principle (Identify/Strengthen)

Step 1: Identify the Question Type
The correct answer will be a principle that "helps to justify" the given reasoning. That makes this an Identify the Principle question that works like a Strengthen question.

Step 2: Untangle the Stimulus

The author describes a plan to build a majestic new subway station. However, that plan doesn't include a certain connection that would be more convenient to commuters. Unfortunately, adding a tunnel for that connection would put the project over budget. So, because the budget can't be changed, the author recommends making the station a little less majestic so that the tunnel can be added.

Step 3: Make a Prediction

In essence, the author wants to sacrifice majesty for the sake of a more convenient experience for commuters. A principle that favors commuter experience over style will justify this decision.

Step 4: Evaluate the Answer Choices

(C) matches the prediction, and is correct.

(A) is a Distortion. The author is only concerned about going over budget. There is no indication that the author wants to spend less. Instead, the author recommends taking some of the money budgeted for majesty and using it for a tunnel instead.

(B) is a Distortion. The author doesn't want the transit authority to merely *consider* the commuter experience. If that were the case, the transit authority could consider a new tunnel but reject the idea. The author doesn't want that. The author wants them to accept the idea and build the tunnel. Furthermore, not *all* potential additions are feasible either, the project still needs to stay within its budget. So, there's no need to consider everything.

(D) is Extreme. The author never argues for abandoning the plans to build a station. The author merely recommends a way to modify the plans.

(E) is an Irrelevant Comparison. The argument is only about the subway station. How that project compares to other projects is of no interest to the author.

12. (B) Assumption (Sufficient)

Step 1: Identify the Question Type

The question asks for something that would fill in the blank at the end of the stimulus. While fill-in-the-blank questions are often Inference questions, the blank in this case is preceded by the Evidence Keyword *since*. That means the blank will be filled with an unstated piece of evidence that, when added, would complete the argument. That's exactly what a Sufficient Assumption question asks for.

Step 2: Untangle the Stimulus

The author mentions that most strokes that are diagnosed occur in the left side of the brain. The author argues that this means right-side strokes are more often undiagnosed.

Step 3: Make a Prediction

Does the greater number of left-side diagnoses really mean that doctors are missing the right-side strokes? Or, is it possible that left-side strokes are just far more common? The author overlooks that possibility, assuming that right-side strokes are about as likely as left-side strokes, and doctors are just failing to diagnose the right-side ones. The correct answer will express that assumption.

Step 4: Evaluate the Answer Choices

(B) is correct. If strokes are equally likely in either side of the brain, then the lack of right-side diagnoses does indicate that the doctors are missing them, as the author argues.

(A) is Out of Scope. The argument is only about strokes. Other health problems are irrelevant.

(C) is Out of Scope. The argument is not about the doctors' accuracy rate. It's about where the stroke occurs when it *is* diagnosed correctly.

(D) is an Irrelevant Comparison. The symptoms of the stroke have no bearing on whether or not the strokes are being diagnosed.

(E) is a Distortion. The argument is not about the number of strokes going undiagnosed, minor or otherwise. It's about which side of the brain is more likely to go undiagnosed.

13. (C) Paradox

Step 1: Identify the Question Type

The question asks for something that "helps to explain" a situation, making this a Paradox question.

Step 2: Untangle the Stimulus

The author is discussing oysters off the coast of Britain. They were dying off, and some native species were on the verge of extinction. While warmer waters were originally blamed, it was eventually determined that a certain chemical (TBT) was responsible for the oyster decline. However, despite removing all the TBT from the area, the population of endangered oysters failed to recover.

Step 3: Make a Prediction

With Paradox questions, it helps to paraphrase the mystery as a question. In this case, if TBT was responsible for killing off the endangered oysters, why didn't their population levels recover when the TBT was completely removed? While it may be difficult to predict an exact solution, it's good to have a general idea what the correct answer will do. The correct answer could show how the TBT had an irreversible long-term effect, or it could show how removing the TBT led to a new problem.

Step 4: Evaluate the Answer Choices

(C) is correct. This states that TBT was also killing off non-native oysters, so removing the TBT would allow them to survive. And if their survival comes at the expense of native oysters, then that would explain why the endangered native oysters can't rebound. The TBT may be gone, but the endangered native oysters are still impacted by the imported oysters.

(A) is Out of Scope. According to the author, it was the TBT, not the warmer waters, that caused the populations to change. So, the water temperature should be irrelevant.

(B) is a 180, at worst. If barnacles and oysters *did* eat the same type of food, then perhaps removing the TBT would mean more barnacles and thus more competition for the oysters. However, having them eat different foods removes the competition angle, and thus fails to explain why the oysters are suffering.

(D) is a 180, at worst. If the TBT was replaced with a different but equally harmful chemical, then that might explain the continuing oyster problem. However, if any replacement chemicals are relatively harmless to the oysters, then the continued population decline is still a mystery.

(E) is an Irrelevant Comparison. If the TBT has been eliminated, then it doesn't matter what type of water makes TBT more deadly.

14. (B) Weaken

Step 1: Identify the Question Type
The question asks for something that "most weakens" the argument, making this a Weaken question.

Step 2: Untangle the Stimulus
Pratt argues that there's really no need for health warnings about removing bats from buildings. The evidence is that, although bats can carry rabies, most bats don't, and they rarely bite.

Step 3: Make a Prediction
If bats are infrequent biters and don't usually carry rabies, that might be a reason not to worry so much about seeing the occasional bat. However, it's a different scenario when you have one living in your home or in the building where you work. Pratt overlooks the possibility that there may be a greater risk if you're living or working constantly in the same building as a bat. Any choice that shows why bats in a building pose a greater health risk would weaken Pratt's argument.

Step 4: Evaluate the Answer Choices
(B) is correct. If rabid bats don't move around as much and are much more aggressive, then that could make it more dangerous if one is in a building. It won't move around, so it will likely stay in the building. And it's more aggressive, and thus more likely to bite.

(A) is a 180. This just adds another reason not to worry about bats. When they do infect something with rabies, it's more likely to be another bat than it is a human.

(C) is an Irrelevant Comparison. The argument is only about bats, so it doesn't matter how bats compare to other animals. Besides, this suggests that bats aren't any more dangerous than other animals, so it offers no reason to question Pratt.

(D) is a 180. This suggests that bats in buildings are even less likely than usual to have rabies, making them safer. That just makes Pratt's argument seem stronger.

(E) is Out of Scope. It doesn't matter if someone is aware of the bite or not. The only concern is whether the bat is likely to bite or not, and this doesn't affect Pratt's point. They're still unlikely to bite, whether we're more aware of it happening or not.

15. (A) Flaw

Step 1: Identify the Question Type
The question asks for a "flaw in the reasoning," making this a Flaw question.

Step 2: Untangle the Stimulus
The author concludes ("it follows") that we can never fully forgive ourselves. The evidence is that complete understanding leads to complete forgiveness, but we can never fully understand ourselves.

Step 3: Make a Prediction
Seeing the first sentence as Formal Logic reveals the logical error. According to the first sentence, understanding is sufficient to bring about forgiveness.

$$\textbf{\textit{If}} \quad \textbf{\textit{understand}} \quad \rightarrow \quad \textbf{\textit{forgive}}$$

However, understanding is not necessary. It is just one condition that could bring about forgiveness. Even without understanding, there could be other conditions that also bring about forgiveness. So, even if we can't understand ourselves, there could still be ways to forgive ourselves. The author overlooks that possibility, and that will be reflected in the correct answer.

Step 4: Evaluate the Answer Choices
(A) is correct. The author treats failing to understand ourselves (which would lead to self-forgiveness) as if it were the only way we could forgive ourselves. There may be other ways.

(B) is a Distortion. If this were true, it would mean the author takes evidence that understanding is needed *before* you can achieve forgiveness and treats it as if understanding is a result that occurs *after* forgiveness. However, the author makes no such confusion. The author only says that understanding leads to forgiveness. The author never suggests that understanding would be a result of forgiveness.

(C) is a Distortion. The evidence is based on what "has been said." However, the conclusion is based on the condition "[i]f so." The author doesn't suggest that the original claim is, in fact, true. The author is just saying what would follow if, *hypothetically*, it were true.

(D) is a Distortion. The author uses the phrase "however desirable," which indicates that the author does *not* ignore desirability. The author is claiming that the conclusion follows whether conditions are desirable or not.

(E) is a Distortion. The author is not saying that one *shouldn't* try because it's difficult. The author is just saying it can't be done.

16. (B) Assumption (Necessary)

Step 1: Identify the Question Type
The question asks for something the argument "depends on assuming," making this a Necessary Assumption question.

Step 2: Untangle the Stimulus
The author concludes ("thereby establishing") that abstract expressionist paintings are aesthetically pleasing. The evidence is that, despite people's complaints about such paintings looking like children's drawings, most participants in a study rated abstract paintings as aesthetically better than paintings done by preschoolers.

Step 3: Make a Prediction
The stimulus is very wordy, but the argument boils down to this: Abstract art looks nice because it looks nicer than what the kids painted. The problem with this argument is one of relativity. Just because X is aesthetically better than Y doesn't mean X is aesthetically good. That's like saying dirt is delicious because it tastes better than spoiled milk. Similarly, just because people find abstract art more pleasing than children's art doesn't mean they actually like the abstract art. It's just relatively better. For this argument to work, the author must assume that people actually find the abstract art pleasing. Put another way, the author assumes people don't find children's art horrible and abstract art just a little less so.

Step 4: Evaluate the Answer Choices
(B) is correct. This suggests that people actually found something pleasing about the kids' art. And if that's true, then the abstract art (which is more pleasing) could also be considered pleasing.

(A) is not necessary. Whether people are better at judging with or without other paintings for comparison, the author's argument that abstract art is aesthetically pleasing still stands.

(C) is a 180, at worst. Whether the paintings were labeled or not, people still preferred the abstract art. In fact, it would seemingly make the argument stronger if this was *not* true. If there were *no* labels, then people wouldn't have been swayed by the labels and would have based their judgments solely on the art itself.

(D) is helpful, but not necessary. It would be nice if the inconsistent people expressed the occasional appreciation of abstract art. However, even if they routinely preferred the kids' art, they're still in the minority. Most people consistently preferred the abstract art. So, the author still has a point no matter what.

(E) is an Irrelevant Comparison. It doesn't matter whether the styles were very similar or very different. All that matters is that most people showed preference for the abstract art.

17. (E) Point At Issue (Agree)

Step 1: Identify the Question Type
There are two speakers in the stimulus, and the correct answer will describe something about which both speakers *agree*. This is a Point at Issue question. While Point at Issue questions usually ask about disagreement, the correct answer here will still rely on recognizing something about which both speakers have an opinion.

Step 2: Untangle the Stimulus
Xavier claims to be unsurprised about the new fast-food place closing. After all, it lacked indoor seating. Miranda agrees that a lack of indoor seating was bound to be a problem, arguing that the bank should have realized that and not lent money for the place.

Step 3: Make a Prediction
Xavier and Miranda both seem to have expected the fast-food place to fail, with both of them citing the lack of indoor seating as a problem. The correct answer should reflect their agreement about the inevitability of closure and/or the problem with limited indoor seating.

Step 4: Evaluate the Answer Choices
(E) is correct. Xavier was not surprised by the place closing, which suggests he realized the risk. And Miranda says the place was "likely to fail," which indicates agreement about that risk.

(A) is Out of Scope for Miranda. While Xavier mentions this directly, Miranda never indicates why the lack of indoor seating was a problem. She *might* agree that people don't like to eat outside, or she might have another reason why the lack of indoor seating was problem. Because it's unknown, there's no way of confirming their agreement on this matter.

(B) is Out of Scope for Xavier and Extreme for Miranda. Xavier doesn't address banks or loans. And Miranda only claims that the lack of indoor seating was a problem on 10th street. Perhaps there are other areas where it would be okay to have no indoor seating.

(C) is Extreme and a Distortion. Xavier and Miranda both claim that the lack of indoor seating was a problem. However, neither one goes so far as to say the place would have succeeded if it *did* have indoor seating. There may been other problems, too.

(D) is a Distortion. The problem is not that the place *had* outdoor seating. The problem is that it *didn't* have indoor seating. The outdoor seating would probably be a non-issue if the place offered indoor seating, as well.

18. (B) Paradox

Step 1: Identify the Question Type
The question asks for something that would "most help to explain" a situation, making this a Paradox question.

Step 2: Untangle the Stimulus
According to the stimulus, Common Eiders at a particular preserve create nests in one of three locations: woody vegetation, wooden boxes, and open grassland. There are about an equal number of nests in each type of area. The author mentions that some Common Eiders will lay their eggs in another bird's nest for maximum protection from predators. In that case, one would expect these birds to choose the most secluded location: woody vegetation. However, they don't. Instead, they mostly lay their eggs in wooden boxes.

Step 3: Make a Prediction
As with any Paradox question, it helps to paraphrase the mystery as a question. If woody vegetation would provide greater protection from predators, why are these birds laying their eggs in the wooden boxes instead? While there may be a few plausible explanations, it's not worth trying to predict any one in particular. The LSAT might choose another. Instead, keep the prediction broad. The correct answer will provide a reason why the birds don't choose nests in woody vegetation and/or why wooden boxes are more often sought out.

Step 4: Evaluate the Answer Choices
(B) is correct. This suggests that Common Eiders may *want* to lay their eggs in the better protected nests, but they just can't find those nests. So, they settle for the next best thing: the nests in wooden boxes.

(A) is Out of Scope. It doesn't matter if the birds eventually wind up building their own nest. The mystery still stands: Until they do build their own nest, why don't they lay their eggs in the location that provides the greatest protection?

(C) is Out of Scope. Even if the birds that did build nests are defensive of their nests (and why wouldn't they be?), that doesn't explain why wooden boxes are more sought out than woody vegetation. Defensive behavior would likely be expected no matter which of the three nest locations were used.

(D) is Out of Scope. It doesn't matter if the habitats were altered by humans or not. The fact remains that woody vegetation provides the best protection, so it's still a mystery why birds are laying eggs in wooden boxes instead.

(E) is Out of Scope. Whether predators are common or not, this doesn't explain why the birds are choosing less protective environments in which to lay their eggs.

19. (D) Flaw

Step 1: Identify the Question Type
The question asks why the "argument is questionable," making this a Flaw question.

Step 2: Untangle the Stimulus
The author concludes that having a medical self-help book at home improves family health. The evidence is an experiment involving 1,000 families. Half were given a self-help book, and the other half were not. The group with the book decreased its average number of doctor visits, while the other group did not. And the author mentions that better family health leads to fewer doctor visits.

Step 3: Make a Prediction
The argument rests on a blatant scope shift. The author's conclusion suggests that families with the self-help book got healthier. However, the evidence just suggests that they went to the doctor less. That doesn't mean they got healthier. Better health *could* have been the reason (as the author mentions). Or, the families may have gotten sick just as often, but they relied on the book instead of going to the doctor. The correct answer should reflect the scope shift and describe how the book may not have actually changed the health of the families.

Step 4: Evaluate the Answer Choices
(D) is correct. Applying the specific content from the stimulus, the flaw is that either of two states of affairs (having the self-help book or better health) could have resulted in the same effect (fewer doctor visits), but the self-help book doesn't necessarily make families healthier, as the author implies.

(A) is a Distortion. This would be the flaw if the author merely concluded that the book was the cause of fewer doctor visits. However, the author doesn't make that claim. Instead, the author commits a different flaw of implying a connection between the book and family health.

(B) is Out of Scope. The conclusion is that a *book* is helpful. Getting information from non-book sources is irrelevant to the argument.

(C) is Out of Scope. The conclusion is that a state of affairs (having a self-help book) leads to one effect (better family health). Even if there are additional effects that the author doesn't mention, those would be irrelevant to the argument.

(E) is a Distortion. This would be a flaw if the author had concluded that the self-help book causes fewer doctor visits. In that case, this answer suggests that having the book and visiting the doctor less may each be caused by an overlooked third factor. However, the author doesn't actually conclude a connection between the book and the doctor visits. The author makes a different unwarranted connection between the book and family health, and this answer fails to address that.

20. (B) Principle (Identify/Strengthen)

Step 1: Identify the Question Type
The question asks for a principle that would "help to justify" the argument, making this an Identify the Principle question that uses the skills of a Strengthen question.

Step 2: Untangle the Stimulus
The politician concludes that the new Ministry of Health should not issue scientific assessments of health issues. The evidence is that political pressures cause the Ministry of Environment to release inaccurate assessments, and the Ministry of Health will be subject to similar political pressures.

Step 3: Make a Prediction
The politician's concern is that political pressures lead to the release of inaccurate information. It is this inaccuracy that forms the basis for the politician's recommendation. So, the politician is acting on the principle that ministries should not issue statements when those statements can be inaccurate.

Step 4: Evaluate the Answer Choices
(B) matches the prediction and is correct.

(A) is Out of Scope. There is no mention of whether or not the scientific assessments are necessary. The argument is based on whether or not those assessments are accurate.

(C) is a Distortion. While this may be another solution to the problem at hand, it's not the solution being proposed by the politician. The politician only recommends an end to releasing inaccurate information, not an end to exercising political pressure.

(D) is a Distortion. The politician's argument is not about suggesting when a ministry *should* issue scientific assessments. The argument is about how certain conditions suggest a ministry should *not* issue scientific assessments.

(E) is a Distortion. While it might be a worthy goal to eventually resist the pressures that lead to inaccurate information, that's not the politician's goal here. This argument is about withholding assessments while the pressures still exist.

21. (B) Flaw

Step 1: Identify the Question Type
The question asks why the argument is "vulnerable to criticism," which is a common indicator of a Flaw question.

Step 2: Untangle the Stimulus
The farmer concludes ([*h*]*ence*) that organic farming should stop spreading to make sure enough food can be produced for Earth's growing population. The evidence is that less food is produced through organic farming, and there wouldn't be enough food produced if every farmer practiced organic farming.

Step 3: Make a Prediction
The problem is that the evidence claims food production would be too low if *all* farmers practiced organic farming. However, that doesn't mean that organic farming has to stop spreading. Perhaps organic farming can continue to spread a little more, and there will still be enough non-organic farming to produce ample food. The farmer's recommendation is a little extreme, assuming that organic farming will inevitably result in underproduction of food. The correct answer will expose this excessive assumption.

Step 4: Evaluate the Answer Choices
(B) is correct. This suggests that organic farming can continue to spread, but there will still be farmers who resist and continue producing ample food through non-organic farming. The farmer in question overlooks this possibility, and that's a flaw.

(A) is an Irrelevant Comparison. The farmer's argument is focused solely on food production, not environmental damage. Whether non-organic farming is slightly more damaging or significantly more damaging, the farmer's argument doesn't change.

(C) is Out of Scope. What might have been true in the past is irrelevant. This argument is based on the growing population and being able to support that population in the future.

(D) is a Distortion. While underproduction of food might occur if all farmers switch to organic farming, the farmer in question doesn't assume it has to reach that extreme level to be a problem. The farmer in question might accept the possibility that problems could still occur even if some farmers refuse to switch. That's why the farmer in question wants to stop the trend now.

(E) is a Distortion. The farmer does mention environmental damage, but that's not presented as a concern. In fact, the farmer seems unconcerned with the environment and only worries about producing enough food for the Earth's population.

22. (D) Inference

Step 1: Identify the Question Type
The correct answer will be something that the given statements "strongly support," making this an Inference question.

Step 2: Untangle the Stimulus

There are a lot of scientific terms here. Don't get lost in the jargon. Simplify the text into easily managed pieces. If a motor nerve gets severed, the severed part can grow back. If the nerve is severed close to the muscle it controls, it will heal quicker than if the nerve is severed further away. Furthermore, nerves need something called a sheath in order to grow back. However, without living nerve tissue, that sheath will start disintegrating after three months.

Step 3: Make a Prediction

The correct answer could be based on anything from the given information. Predicting the exact answer can be difficult, if not impossible. Instead, evaluate the choices against the stimulus, being sure to avoid answers that stray from the scope or use extreme language.

Step 4: Evaluate the Answer Choices

(D) is correct. According to the last line, the sheath needed to regrow nerves will start disintegrating after three months without living nerve tissue. So, if living nerve tissue can be implanted, that might help in cases that need the extra time.

(A) is not supported. The only problem the author addresses is nerve repairs that require more than three months. However, if the severing point is really close and only needs about a month to regrow, then the regrowth should be equally likely at regular speed or double speed.

(B) is not supported. While it's suggested that supplying live tissue can help prevent disintegration from happening in the first place, that doesn't mean that disintegration can be stopped or slowed down if it does occur.

(C) is Extreme. Three months is only a problem if there's no living nerve tissue underneath the sheath. If some living nerve tissue can still be found underneath the sheath, then the sheath may be able to go longer than three months before disintegrating. Thus, there's no reason to say function *cannot* be restored in that time.

(E) is Out of Scope. The very first sentence suggests that nerves could regenerate on their own when severed. There is no indication that any surgery would be required.

23. (D) Parallel Reasoning

Step 1: Identify the Question Type

The question asks for an argument with reasoning "most similar" to the reasoning in the stimulus. That makes this a Parallel Reasoning question.

Step 2: Untangle the Stimulus

The author concludes that male boto dolphins carry weeds and sticks as part of a mating ritual and not, as originally thought, for play. The evidence is that, if it were for play, then females and children would do it, too. However, they don't.

Step 3: Make a Prediction

The entire argument is based on using a contrapositive to rule out a hypothesis. If a certain hypothesis were true (carrying weeds and sticks is done for play), then a certain result would be expected (all dolphins would do it). However, the expected result is *not* observed (only males are seen doing it). So, by contrapositive, the author concludes that the hypothesis is false (it's not for play), and an alternative is likely ("more likely to be a mating display"). The correct answer will use the same contrapositive technique.

Step 4: Evaluate the Answer Choices

(D) is a match. Like the original, the argument claims that, if a hypothesis were true (construction on schedule), a result would be expected (completed foundation). The result is not observed (incomplete foundation), so the conclusion denies the hypothesis (it's delayed, i.e., not on schedule), and an alternative is likely ("probably behind schedule").

(A) does not match. This uses the Formal Logic improperly. Here, the logic is this: If there's a lot traffic, Phyllis would be late. However, instead of doing the contrapositive, the author illicitly negates the logic, claiming that little traffic would lead to Phyllis being on time. There are other issues, but only one error is needed to eliminate a wrong answer.

(B) does not match. It does not use a contrapositive. Further, it does not deny a hypothesis. Instead, this argument confirms any hypotheses presented (e.g., finding a disease, cutting the tree down).

(C) does not match. This improperly reverses the Formal Logic instead of creating a proper contrapositive. Further, the hypothesis provided (Roy cancelling his trip) is confirmed here instead of denied.

(E) does not match. This does not use a contrapositive. Further, this argument suggests that any hypothesis (e.g., Tamika making a sale and celebrating) "will probably" happen. It doesn't deny the hypothesis, as the original argument does.

24. (E) Method of Argument

Step 1: Identify the Question Type

The phrase "proceeds by" indicates a Method of Argument question. The correct answer will describe how the author argues, i.e., what argumentative technique is used.

Step 2: Untangle the Stimulus

The author concludes ([*t*]*herefore*) that appearance alone does not determine whether or not something is art. The evidence is that Andy Warhol's work *Brillo Boxes* looks exactly like an actual pile of Brillo boxes, yet Warhol's pile is considered art while the actual pile is not.

Step 3: Make a Prediction

The correct answer will describe the author's method without getting too caught up in the details. In this case, the author is using an observation about appearances (two things look the same, but only one is considered art) to deny a claim about art (the author denies appearance is enough to determine art). It can be expected that the correct answer will be consistent with this idea.

Step 4: Evaluate the Answer Choices

(E) is correct, even if not written as expected. First, apply the content of the argument to see why this is accurate. The thesis here (that the author refutes in the conclusion) is that appearance alone determines whether something is art. If that thesis were true, it would be impossible to distinguish between Warhol's *Brillo Boxes* and an actual pile of Brillo boxes. However, that's not impossible—it's actually true that a distinction can be made. It all lines up, making this choice correct. So, what about the fact that the author goes one step further and actually *denies* the thesis? Admittedly, it's highly unusual for the LSAT to leave something like that out. However, this is the only choice that matches any aspect of the author's technique, and thus accurately describes a way in which the argument proceeds. The remaining choices are all inaccurate.

(A) is Out of Scope. The only things compared are Warhol's *Brillo Boxes* and an actual pile of boxes. However, there are two problems with this choice. First, the property in question is whether or not these piles are art. The author only discusses what is believed about that property—that Warhol's pile is art and the actual pile is not. There is no claim that Warhol's pile actually is art. Second, the author never highlights the differences that help make the distinction. Why only Warhol's pile is considered art is still a mystery.

(B) is a Distortion. If there's an opposing argument, it's that appearances alone determine whether something is art. However, there's no ambiguity about that. The author argues it's wrong and provides a clear counterexample.

(C) is a 180. The author says they're *not* the same. One is art, and the other is not.

(D) is a Distortion. The author denies the theory that appearance alone determines whether something is art. However, the author disputes that by presenting a counterexample, not by questioning any assumptions.

25. (A) Parallel Flaw

Step 1: Identify the Question Type

The question asks for an argument that is "most similar" to the one in the stimulus, and they will both contain the same "flawed reasoning." That makes this a Parallel Flaw question.

Step 2: Untangle the Stimulus

The author first mentions Stallworth, who claims to support building a new community center. The author then mentions Henning. If Henning also supported that proposal, it would have been approved. However, it wasn't approved. So, the author concludes that Henning contradicted himself and didn't support the proposal.

Step 3: Make a Prediction

The author correctly uses the contrapositive. If Henning supported the proposal, it would have been approved. It wasn't approved, so Henning doesn't support the proposal. So, where's the flaw? The flaw comes with the very last line: "despite his claims to the contrary." The author never said that Henning claimed to support the proposal. It was *Stallworth* that made that claim. That's the flaw in this argument—the author gets mixed up and blames one person for saying something that was actually said by someone else. The correct answer will commit the same flaw.

Step 4: Evaluate the Answer Choices

(A) is correct. Like the original argument, this correctly uses a contrapositive: If the accident was on Aylmer street, Morgan wouldn't have seen it from the kitchen; Morgan did see it from the kitchen, so it wasn't on Aylmer. However, also like the original, this author gets mixed up and blames the newspaper for saying the wrong thing when it was TV news that claimed it was on Aylmer street.

(B) does not match. This assigns blame to the government based on data from a private institute. There's no mistake of confusing who said what.

(C) does not match. This claims that two people have differing opinions and that if one is right, the other must be wrong. This may be flawed because both people could be right (it's possible that there's no imminent danger but the land is still unsuitable for other reasons). However, that's not the same flaw as the original argument.

(D) does not match. This makes a judgment on Harris, and perhaps an unnecessarily harsh one. However, there's no flaw in mistaking who said what.

(E) does not match. This questions one set of statistics by citing another set. This may be flawed due to overlooked possibilities (i.e., maybe unemployment is better overall even if manufacturing jobs have declined). However, that's not the same "who-said-what?" flaw committed in the original argument.

Section II: Logic Games

Game 1: Lectures at a Two-Day Conference

Q#	Question Type	Correct	Difficulty
1	Acceptability	B	★
2	"If" / Could Be True EXCEPT	C	★
3	Must Be False (CANNOT Be True)	A	★
4	"If" / Must Be True	E	★
5	Must Be False (CANNOT Be True)	A	★
6	Rule Substitution	A	★★★★

Game 2: Art Auction

Q#	Question Type	Correct	Difficulty
7	Earliest	D	★
8	Must Be False (CANNOT Be True)	C	★
9	Supply the If	A	★
10	How Many	C	★
11	"If" / How Many	D	★
12	"If" / Must Be True	E	★★

Game 3: Mining Company Engineering Team

Q#	Question Type	Correct	Difficulty
13	Partial Acceptability	B	★
14	Must Be True	E	★★★
15	Must Be True	D	★★
16	"If" / Could Be True	C	★★
17	"If" / Could Be True	D	★★★

Game 4: Medical Clinic Shifts

Q#	Question Type	Correct	Difficulty
18	Acceptability	D	★
19	"If" / Must Be True	A	★
20	"If" / Could Be True EXCEPT	C	★
21	"If" / Could Be True	E	★★
22	"If" / Must Be True	D	★★
23	Could Be True EXCEPT	E	★★

Game 1: Lectures at a Two-Day Conference

Step 1: Overview

Situation: Speakers giving lectures at a two-day conference

Entities: Six speakers (Jacobs, Kennedy, Lewis, Martin, Navarro, Ota)

Action: Distribution/Matching Hybrid. Determine the day on which each speaker lectures (Distribution), and determine the time at which the lecture is given (Matching). The use of times seems to suggest a Sequencing element. However, there are no rules or questions that mention ordering (e.g., no "before" or "after" language), so sequencing skills are not tested here.

Limitations: Each speaker lectures once, and only one speaker will lecture in each time slot.

Step 2: Sketch

List the speakers by initial. Then, set up a table with two columns, one for each day (Thursday and Friday). In each column, draw three slots, one for each time (1:00, 2:00, and 3:00). Make sure the slots for each time are lined up.

JKLMNO

	Th	Fr
1	—	—
2	—	—
3	—	—

Step 3: Rules

Rule 1 establishes Jacobs at 1:00, but does not indicate which day. Draw J next to the 1:00 row in the sketch.

Rule 2 places Martin and Navarro on the same day. That could happen on either day, so make a note of this (e.g., "M, N = same day") to the side.

Rule 3 requires Lewis and Ota to lecture on different days. With only two days available, one of them must lecture on Thursday, and the other one will lecture on Friday. Add "L/O" below each column in the sketch.

Rule 4 provides some Formal Logic. If Lewis lectures on Friday, it must be at 1:00. By contrapositive, if Lewis does not lecture at 1:00 (i.e., he lectures at 2:00 or 3:00), Lewis cannot lecture on Friday (which means Lewis will lecture on Thursday).

$$\frac{Fr}{L} \rightarrow 1L$$

$$2/3\ L \rightarrow \frac{Th}{L}$$

This rule could be incorporated directly into the sketch. If Lewis lectured on Friday, it would have to be at 1:00, which means Lewis cannot lecture at 2:00 or 3:00 on Friday. On Thursday, Lewis can lecture at any time. So, adding "~L" under the 2:00 and 3:00 positions on Friday would be enough to ensure the rule is followed.

Step 4: Deductions

The most important deduction in this game comes from combining Rules 2 and 3. The block of Martin and Navarro (Rule 2) could lecture either day. They will take up any two of that day's slots. By Rule 3, the third slot on that day would have to be Lewis or Ota. So, one of the days will consist of Martin, Navarro, and either Lewis or Ota (M, N, L/O). That means the other day would have to consist of the remaining speakers: Jacobs, Kennedy, and either Lewis or Ota (J, K, L/O). This shows that Jacobs and Kennedy will always lecture on the same day.

With only two days, it is possible to set up Limited Options. In the first option, Martin and Navarro (along with Lewis or Ota) will lecture on Thursday, with Jacobs and Kennedy (along with Lewis or Ota) on Friday. In the second option, Martin and Navarro (with Lewis or Ota) will lecture on Friday, with Jacobs and Kennedy (along with Lewis or Ota) on Thursday.

In the first option, Jacobs has to lecture at 1:00 (Rule 1), so add J to the first slot on Friday. Because of that, Lewis cannot lecture on Friday (Rule 4), as the 1:00 slot is now filled. So, Lewis will lecture on Thursday, which means Ota will lecture on Friday with Kennedy. Ota and Kennedy will lecture at 2:00 and 3:00, in either order. For Thursday, the speakers will be Lewis, Martin, and Navarro, in any order.

I)	Th	Fr
1	L/M/N	J
2	L/M/N	K/O
3	L/M/N	O/K

In the second option, Jacobs has to lecture at 1:00 (Rule 1), so add J to the first slot on Thursday. Unfortunately, that's where the deductions end. Lewis and Ota could each speak on either day, and there are no restrictions on the times for Kennedy, Martin, or Navarro.

II)	Th	Fr
1	J	—
2	—	— ~L
3	—	— ~L
	K	M
	L/O	N
		O/L

Step 5: Questions

1. (B) Acceptability

As with any Acceptability question, go through the rules one at a time and eliminate choices that violate the rules.

(E) violates Rule 1 by assigning Jacobs to a 2:00 lecture. **(C)** violates Rule 2 by assigning Martin and Navarro to different days. **(D)** violates Rule 3 by assigning Lewis and Ota to the same day. **(A)** violates Rule 4 by assigning Lewis to Friday but not at 1:00. That leaves **(B)** as the only one that follows the rules, and thus the correct answer.

2. (C) "If" / Could Be True EXCEPT

For this question, Martin will lecture at 1:00. By Rule 1, so does Jacobs. That means the 1:00 lectures will be Jacobs and Martin, each on either day. With the 1:00 lectures filled, Lewis cannot speak at 1:00. So, by the contrapositive of Rule 4, Lewis cannot lecture on Friday. That makes **(C)** the correct answer.

3. (A) Must Be False (CANNOT Be True)

The question asks for a pair of speakers that cannot lecture on the same day. That means the incorrect choices will list speakers who could lecture on the same day.

Martin and Navarro definitely lecture on the same day, and the third person that day has to be Lewis or Ota (Rule 3). That means Jacobs and Kennedy would have to lecture on a different day. So, neither Jacobs nor Kennedy can lecture on the same day as either Martin or Navarro. That makes **(A)** the correct answer. Navarro must be on one day, with Jacobs on the other. The remaining choices all list either Lewis or Ota, each of whom could lecture with any of the remaining four speakers.

4. (E) "If" / Must Be True

For this question, Kennedy will lecture at 3:00 on Friday. That means Martin and Navarro, along with Lewis or Ota, must lecture on Thursday. So, the rest of Friday will consist of Jacobs and either Lewis or Ota. Jacobs has to lecture at 1:00, which leaves only the 2:00 position. Lewis can't speak at 2:00 on Friday (Rule 4), so the 2:00 lecture on Friday must be Ota. That means Lewis will lecture on Thursday, along with Martin and Navarro, in any order. (Note that this works only in the first option of the Limited Options, which could have saved a few steps here.)

	Th	Fr
I)		
1	__	J
2	__	O
3	__	K

L/M/N

With Ota lecturing at 2:00 on Friday, **(E)** is the correct answer.

5. (A) Must Be False (CANNOT Be True)

The question asks for a speaker who cannot lecture at 1:00. That means the remaining entities list speakers who can lecture at 1:00. Because Martin and Navarro have to speak on the same day (Rule 2), along with Lewis or Ota (Rule 3), Jacobs and Kennedy will speak together on a different day. On that day, Jacobs has to speak at 1:00, so Kennedy will be forced to speak at a different time (2:00 or 3:00). That makes **(A)** the correct answer.

For the record, the sketch for the first option and/or the sketch for the fourth question both show that Lewis, Martin, and Navarro speak on Thursday, with each one available at 1:00. That's enough to eliminate **(B)**, **(C)**, and **(D)**. Ota has no time restriction. So, as long as Ota is assigned a different day from Jacobs (which could happen in the second option), Ota can certainly lecture at 1:00, that eliminates **(E)**.

6. (A) Rule Substitution

The correct answer will be a new rule that could serve as an exact replacement for Rule 3 (which places Lewis and Ota on different days). In other words, it will create the exact same restriction without adding any new restrictions.

Start with **(A)**. By Rule 2, Martin and Navarro have to lecture on the same day. So, if Jacobs and Kennedy have to lecture on the same day, it must be a different day from Martin and Navarro, as only three speakers lecture each day. By putting Jacobs and Kennedy together, one day will have Martin and Navarro, and the other will have Jacobs and Kennedy. That leaves only one slot on each day, one each for Lewis and Ota. That means Lewis and Ota must be split up, just as the original rule required. And the combination of Jacobs and Kennedy was always true in the original setup. So, **(A)** would create the exact conditions of the original rules, making that the correct answer. For the record:

(B) and **(C)** are too restrictive, and thus can be eliminated. The original rules never required Ota to lecture on the same day as anyone in particular. **(D)** and **(E)** are both consistent with the original deductions. However, separating Jacobs and Martin would not be enough to separate Lewis and Ota. It would still be possible to have Jacobs, Lewis, and Ota on one day, with Martin, Navarro, and Kennedy on the other. That eliminates **(D)**. Similarly, separating Kennedy and Navarro would not necessarily separate Lewis and Ota. It would still be possible to have Kennedy, Lewis, and Ota one day, with Jacobs, Martin, and Navarro on the other. That eliminates **(E)**.

Game 2: Art Auction

Step 1: Overview

Situation: Paintings being auctioned

Entities: Six paintings (one each by Joysmith, Kahlo, Nieto, Rothko, Sugimoto, Villa)

Action: Strict Sequencing. Determine the order in which the paintings will be auctioned.

Limitations: Each painting will be auctioned, with each one auctioned separately. That makes this standard one-to-one sequencing.

Step 2: Sketch

List the paintings by the artists' initials, and set up a horizontal row of six numbered slots.

JKNRSV

—— —— —— —— —— ——
1   2   3   4   5   6

Step 3: Rules

Rule 1 prevents the Joysmith and the Villa from being consecutive, in either order. Make a note of this to the side.

Rule 2 sets up a loose sequence. The Villa, the Kahlo, and the Sugimoto will be auctioned in that order, though not necessarily consecutively.

V...K...S

Rule 3 limits the Nieto to being auctioned second or third. Place "N" by the sketch with arrows pointing to the second and third positions.

Rule 4 sets up another loose sequence. The Rothko will be auctioned at some point before the Nieto.

R...N

Step 4: Deductions

The Nieto is a Duplication. Rule 3 limits the Nieto to second or third. By Rule 4, the Rothko must precede the Nieto. So, depending on when the Nieto is auctioned, the Rothko could only be auctioned first or second. Add "R" to the sketch with arrows pointing to the first and second positions.

With the Rothko and the Nieto taking up two of the first three auctions, there's only room for one other painting in the first half. That final painting cannot be the Kahlo or the Sugimoto, which have to wait until after the Villa is auctioned (Rule 2). So, the Kahlo and Sugimoto have to be auctioned in the

second half, with the Kahlo auctioned fourth or fifth, and the Sugimito auctioned either fifth or sixth.

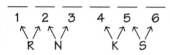

That leaves the Joysmith and the Villa. One of them will be among the first three paintings, along with the Nieto and the Rothko. The other will be among the last three paintings, along with the Kahlo and Sugimoto. This could be used to set up Limited Options. There are also opportunities for Limited Options based on some of the more restricted entities (including the Nieto). They are certainly worth considering, but the game can be managed effectively with or without them.

Step 5: Questions

7. (D) Earliest

The question asks for the earliest point at which the Kahlo could be auctioned. The Kahlo must be auctioned after the Villa, so it cannot be auctioned first. If the Villa was first, then the Rothko and the Nieto would be second and third, respectively (Rules 3 and 4). So, the Kahlo would have to wait until the fourth auction. And similar restrictions would happen if the Villa were second or third. So, the Kahlo cannot be auctioned any earlier than fourth, making **(D)** the correct answer.

8. (C) Must Be False (CANNOT Be True)

The correct answer to this question will be a time when the Joysmith cannot be auctioned. The incorrect choices will be times when the Joysmith could be auctioned.

The only restriction on the Joysmith is that it cannot be auctioned consecutively with the Villa. That's not enough, on the surface, to eliminate any particular position. However, instead of testing each answer position individually, look for a way to test multiple choices simultaneously.

By Rules 3 and 4, the Rothko and the Nieto must take up two of the first three positions. The remaining position could be occupied by the Joysmith or the Villa. If the remaining position was occupied by the Joysmith, then the fourth, fifth, and six auctions would have to be the Villa, the Kahlo, and the Sugimoto, in that order.

—— —— —— V K S
1 2 3 4 5 6

J;R...N

In that case, the Joysmith could be auctioned first or second, but could never be auctioned third without violating Rule 1. That makes **(C)** the correct answer. For the record, the other option would have the Villa occupying one of the first three slots along with the Rothko and the Nieto. In that case, the Villa could be auctioned first, and the Joysmith could be auctioned in any of the last three positions: fourth, fifth, or sixth.

9. (A) Supply the If

The correct answer will be a new condition that will force the Kahlo to be auctioned fourth. By the deductions, the Kahlo can only be auctioned fourth or fifth. If anything else was auctioned fifth, that would guarantee the Kahlo being auctioned fourth. That makes **(A)** the correct answer.

Without the deduction, the answers could still be tested one by one. Luckily, **(A)** works right away. Placing the Joysmith fifth means that in order to leave two open spots for the Kahlo and Sugimoto in the sequence of Rule 2, the Villa must be first, second, or third. In order to have the Nieto precede the Rothko (Rule 4), and keep the Nieto second or third (Rule 3), the two of them must join the Villa in the first three. This definitively places the Kahlo fourth and the Sugimoto sixth to follow the sequence of Rule 2.

10. (C) How Many

The question asks for the number of paintings that could be auctioned fifth. Start by eliminating the paintings that certainly cannot be fifth. By Rule 3, the Nieto can only be auctioned second or third. And By Rule 4, the Rothko has to be auctioned before that. So, neither of those could be auctioned fifth.

That leaves the Joysmith, the Kahlo, the Sugimoto, and the Villa. By Rule 2, the Villa has to be auctioned before both the Kahlo and the Sugimoto, so the latest it could be auctioned is fourth, never fifth. Any of the remaining three—the Joysmith, the Kahlo, or the Sugimoto—could be fifth, making **(C)** the correct answer.

To confirm without a lot of testing, the sketches for the last two questions confirm that the Kahlo and the Sugimoto could be fifth. And in the second question, the incorrect choices list positions when Joysmith *could* be auctioned, and those choices include fifth.

11. (D) "If" / How Many

For this question, the Villa is auctioned fourth. That means the Kahlo and the Sugimoto must be auctioned fifth and sixth, respectively (Rule 2). That leaves the Joysmith, the Nieto, and the Rothko. The Joysmith cannot be next to the Villa (Rule 1), and the Rothko has to be auctioned before the Nieto (Rule 4), so only the Nieto could be auctioned third. The Joysmith and the Rothko would then be auctioned first and second, in either order.

$$
\begin{array}{cccccc}
\underline{J/R} & \underline{R/J} & \underline{N} & \underline{V} & \underline{K} & \underline{S} \\
1 & 2 & 3 & 4 & 5 & 6
\end{array}
$$

In that case, the second auction could only be the Joysmith or the Rothko. That's two possible paintings, making **(D)** the correct answer.

12. (E) "If" / Must Be True

For this question, the Sugimoto will be auctioned earlier than the Joysmith. By Rule 2, the Villa and the Kahlo have to be auctioned before the Sugimoto. So, in relative order, the auction must have the Villa, the Kahlo, the Sugimito, then the Joysmith.

By Rules 3 and 4, the Rothko and the Nieto, in that order, will be two of the first three paintings auctioned. The remaining painting would have to be the Villa, leaving the Kahlo, the Sugimoto, and the Joysmith to be auctioned fourth, fifth, and sixth, in that order.

$$
\begin{array}{cccccc}
\underline{} & \underline{} & \underline{} & \underline{K} & \underline{S} & \underline{J} \\
1 & 2 & 3 & 4 & 5 & 6
\end{array}
$$
$$
\underbrace{}
$$
$$
V; R \ldots N
$$

With that, Kahlo is definitely auctioned fourth, making **(E)** the correct answer. The remaining choices are all possible but need not be true.

Game 3: Mining Company Engineering Team

Step 1: Overview
Situation: A mining company sending an engineering team to different mines

Entities: Two mines (Grayson and Krona)

Action: Strict Sequencing. Determine the months (in a sequential schedule) during which the engineering team will work at the mines.

Limitations: The schedule consists of nine months, from March to November. The team will work at each mine for three months each, for a total of six out the nine months. In the remaining three months, the team will work at the company headquarters.

Step 2: Sketch
The basic framework will be nine consecutive slots, labeled for the nine months. Due to the many duplicated initials (e.g., March and May, April and August, June and July), it's worth either using abbreviations (Mar, Apr, May, etc.) or the corresponding month numbers (3, 4, 5, etc.) instead of just single-letter initials. As for the entities, Grayson and Krona will be assigned three times apiece, so list each three times. The remaining three months will involve working at headquarters, so add three of those to the entity list, too. Find a way to distinguish between the mines and the headquarters—perhaps two letters for each mine, but a single letter for the headquarters. That sets up a total of nine entities, one for each month.

GrGrGr KrKrKr HHH

3	4	5	6	7	8	9	10	11

Admittedly, this is a bulkier sketch than most logic games will require. However, looking for shortcuts can lead to an ambiguous or unclear sketch, which could wind up leading to wasted time in the long run. Always favor accuracy over speed.

Step 3: Rules
Rule 1 requires the team to work at headquarters for at least one month in between working at different mines. In other words, the team can never work one month at Grayson and then the next month at Krona, or vice versa.

Gr ~~Kr~~

Kr ~~Gr~~

Rule 2 prevents the team from working at the same mine for more than two months in a row. In other words, the team will not work all three months at either mine in three consecutive months. Make a note of this to the side.

Gr ~~Gr~~ ~~Gr~~

Kr ~~Kr~~ ~~Kr~~

Rules 3 and 4 establish two visits: Grayson in August and Krona in October. Add "Gr" and "Kr" to the Aug (8) and Oct (10) slots, respectively.

Step 4: Deductions
The first major deduction comes from the Established Entities of G and K in August and October. By Rule 1, the team must work at headquarters in between those visits, so add "H" to Sep (9).

Beyond that, this game is driven by numbers. The team cannot work at the same mine for three months in a row. At most, it can work two months in a row before it has to work elsewhere. Then, it would have to go back to that mine at a later date to complete the third month. So, the team has to work at least two separate shifts at each mine, for a minimum of four shifts.

Further, after working at one mine, the team cannot just switch to the other mine. So, the team always has to go back and work at headquarters between shifts. However, the team will only work at headquarters three times. To have at least four separate shifts at the mines with only three months in between at headquarters, the schedule has to be arranged like so:

Mine...H...Mine...H...Mine...H...Mine

There is no other way to work the numbers. So, the team must work exactly four shifts at the mines. There will be two shifts at Grayson—one that lasts one month (Gr) and one that lasts two months (GrGr). And there will be two shifts at Krona—one that lasts one month (Kr) and one that lasts two months (KrKr). The three months at headquarters will happen in between these shifts.

Then, because the work at headquarters will be in the middle, the first month (March) and the last month (November) have to be spent at a mine. The March mine could be either Grayson or Krona. However, with the team working at Krona in October, November can only be spent at Krona. And that would be the two-month shift at Krona. The one-month shift at Krona can occur anywhere else in the schedule, except for July (which would make it consecutive with a shift at Grayson). July could be spent at Grayson, or it could be one of the remaining months at headquarters.

Gr/Kr				Gr/H	Gr	H	Kr	Kr
3	4	5	6	7	8	9	10	11

Step 5: Questions

13. (B) Partial Acceptability

Even though the choices only list five of the nine months, it's still best to start with the rules. Eliminate answers that directly violate the rules. Consider the unlisted months only if more than one answer remains.

(E) violates Rule 1 by having the team work at Krona in July followed by Grayson in August, with no work at headquarters in between. **(A)** violates Rule 2 by having the team work at Grayson in three consecutive months (June, July, and August). **(C)** violates Rule 3 by having the team work at Krona instead of Grayson in August. And **(D)** violates Rule 4 by having the team work at Grayson instead of Krona in October. Without having to consider the unlisted months, **(B)** is the only answer remaining and is thus the correct answer.

14. (E) Must Be True

The correct answer will be a month in which the team must work at Krona. Through the deductions, it was determined that the team must work at Krona in November, making **(E)** the correct answer.

Without the deduction, this question could also be quickly answered by waiting for the new sketches from the final two questions of the set. The only month that Krona is definitely placed for each sketch (besides October) is November.

15. (D) Must Be True

The correct answer to this question must be true. By Rules 3 and 4, the team will work at Grayson and Krona in August and

October, respectively. By Rule 1, these shifts must be separated by a return to headquarters. So, the team must work at headquarters in September, making **(D)** the correct answer.

Also, just like the previous question, this one can be answered by using the sketch from another question. In the sketch for the next question (the second to last of the set), **(A)**, **(B)**, and **(C)** all could be true; **(E)** must be false, leaving **(D)** as the only one that must be true.

16. (C) "If" / Could Be True

For this question, the team works at Grayson in May. The team still needs to work one more month at Grayson and one more at Krona. By Rule 1, with Grayson in May and August, the remaining month at Krona cannot be April, June, or July. Thus, it must occur in March. With Krona in March and Grayson in May, the team must work at headquarters in between in April. For June and July, the team will work at Grayson one month and at headquarters for the other.

Kr	H	Gr	Gr/H	H/Gr	Gr	H	Kr	Kr
3	4	5	6	7	8	9	10	11

With that, only **(C)** is possible and is thus the correct answer.

17. (D) "If" / Could Be True

For this question, the team will work at Grayson in July. The team also works at Grayson in August (Rule 3). Because the team cannot work at Grayson for three months in a row (Rule 2), and the team cannot work at Krona the month immediately before working at Grayson (Rule 1), the team must work at headquarters in June. That leaves one more month at Grayson and one more month at Krona. They cannot be consecutive, so they will be separated by the third month at headquarters. So, the team will work at Grayson and Krona in March and May, in either order, and work at headquarters in April.

Gr/Kr	H	Kr/Gr	H	Gr	Gr	H	Kr	Kr
3	4	5	6	7	8	9	10	11

With that, only **(D)** is possible and thus the correct answer.

Game 4: Medical Clinic Shifts

Step 1: Overview
Situation: Doctors being assigned shifts at a medical clinic

Entities: Six doctors (Graham, Herrera, Koppel, Leedom, Nelson, Park)

Action: Strict Sequencing. Determine the order in which the doctors will be assigned shifts during the week.

Limitations: The weekly schedule consists of seven days (Sunday through Saturday), but there are only six doctors. Each doctor has to work at least once, and there must be one doctor each day. So, five of the doctors will work one day, and the remaining doctor will work two days.

Step 2: Sketch
List the doctors by initial and set up a horizontal set of seven slots, one for each day. Because some days have identical initials (e.g., Saturday and Sunday; Tuesday and Thursday), consider using abbreviations to avoid ambiguity.

GHKLNP

<u>Su</u> <u>Mo</u> <u>Tu</u> <u>We</u> <u>Th</u> <u>Fr</u> <u>Sa</u>

Step 3: Rules
Rule 1 establishes the days for the one doctor assigned twice: Sunday and Saturday. Unfortunately, it's still not clear who that doctor is. So, draw an equal sign with arrows pointing to Sunday and Saturday, or make a note of this in shorthand (e.g., "Su = Sa").

Rule 2 limits Graham to one day. Make a note by "G" in the entity list (e.g., a "1" above the "G") or write a note to the side (e.g., "Exactly 1 G").

Rule 3 creates a Block of Entities. Graham and Koppel must be assigned to consecutive days, in either order.

GK or KG

Note that Graham will only be assigned once, and must be consecutive with Koppel. However, Koppel can still be assigned to two days, and Graham would have to be assigned consecutively to only one of those days. The other "K" would be by itself.

Rule 4 prevents Herrera and Nelson from being assigned consecutive days, in either order.

Rule 5 establishes Park on Tuesday. Add "P" to the Tuesday slot in the sketch.

Step 4: Deductions
Because one doctor has to be repeated, numbers will be important. By Rule 2, Graham is only assigned once. And the repeated doctor has to be assigned to Sunday and Saturday (Rule 1). So, because Park is assigned to Tuesday (Rule 5), Park will not be repeated. However, that still leaves Herrera, Koppel, Leedom, and Nelson, any of whom could be repeated.

In addition, the one entity duplicated in the rules is Graham. Graham is only assigned once (Rule 2) and thus cannot be the doctor assigned to Sunday and Saturday. Add "~G" under those days in the sketch. Whenever Graham is assigned, Koppel will be assigned a consecutive day. However, there are still four days available for Graham (Monday, Wednesday, Thursday, and Friday), which leaves a lot of options for Koppel.

So, this game provides no major deductions. However, that can be expected when four of the six questions are New-"If" questions. That often indicates that the rules don't offer very much and the game is more reliant on adding additional conditions. As one final note, Leedom is not mentioned in any of the rules and is thus a Floater.

Step 5: Questions

18. (D) Acceptability
As with any standard Acceptability question, go through the rules one at a time and eliminate choices as they violate those rules.

(B) violates Rule 1 by assigning different doctors to Sunday and Saturday. Nothing violates Rule 2. **(A)** violates Rule 3 by failing to assign Koppel next to Graham. **(C)** violates Rule 4 by having Herrera and Nelson on consecutive days. **(E)** violates Rule 5 by assigning Park to Monday instead of Tuesday. **(D)** doesn't violate any of the rules and is thus the correct answer.

19. (A) "If" / Must Be True

For this question, Nelson is assigned to Sunday. That means Nelson is also assigned to Saturday (Rule 1). Everyone else will be assigned just once. Graham and Koppel must be consecutive (Rule 3), so they can only be on Wednesday and Thursday or Thursday and Friday (which guarantees one of them is on Thursday). Herrera cannot be consecutive with Nelson (Rule 4), so Herrera cannot be assigned to Monday or Friday. That leaves Wednesday or Thursday. Herrera cannot go on Thursday without breaking up the Graham/Koppel block, so Herrera must be assigned to Wednesday, leaving Graham and Koppel on Thursday and Friday, in either order. That leaves Monday open for the one remaining doctor: Leedom.

N	L	P	H	G/K	K/G	N
Su	Mo	Tu	We	Th	Fr	Sa

With Herrera established on Wednesday, **(A)** is correct.

20. (C) "If" / Could Be True EXCEPT

For this question, Koppel is assigned to Thursday. That means Koppel will only be assigned once (Rule 1). So, the duplicated doctor can only be Herrera, Leedom, or Nelson. Herrera and Nelson are restricted exactly the same, so there are really only two options to consider. Draw them both out.

In the first option, Herrera or Nelson will be the doctor assigned to Sunday and Saturday. Because Herrera and Nelson cannot be assigned to consecutive days (Rule 4), the one assigned once cannot be on Monday or Friday. That doctor will have to be assigned to Wednesday. To be consecutive with Koppel (Rule 3), Graham will have to be on Friday, leaving Monday for Leedom.

I) H/N	L	P	N/H	K	G	H/N
Su	Mo	Tu	We	Th	Fr	Sa

In the second option, Leedom will be the doctor assigned to Sunday and Saturday. In that case, Herrera and Nelson will definitely be split. One of them will have to be assigned to Monday, as Graham has to be consecutive with Koppel. The other will work on Wednesday or Friday, whichever day goes unassigned to Graham.

II) L	H/N	P	G/N/H	K	G/N/H	L
Su	Mo	Tu	We	Th	Fr	Sa

Considering both options, all of the choices are possible except for **(C)**. Leedom, despite being a Floater, is limited to either Monday or Sunday and Saturday. Leedom never appears on Wednesday. **(C)** is the correct answer.

21. (E) "If" / Could Be True

For this question, Leedom is assigned to Wednesday. That means the doctor assigned to Sunday and Saturday can only be Herrera, Koppel, or Nelson. However, if it was Herrera or Nelson, that would only leave Thursday and Friday for Graham and Koppel to be consecutive (Rule 3). That would force Herrera and Nelson to be consecutive on Sunday and Monday, thus violating Rule 4. So, the doctor on Sunday and Saturday must be Koppel. Graham would have to be assigned to Monday or Friday. However, if Graham were on Monday, Herrera and Nelson would be consecutive on Thursday and Friday, again violating Rule 4. So, Graham has to be assigned to Friday. Herrera and Nelson will be assigned to Monday and Thursday, in either order.

K	H/N	P	L	N/H	G	K
Su	Mo	Tu	We	Th	Fr	Sa

In that case, only **(E)** is possible and thus the correct answer.

22. (D) "If" / Must Be True

For this question, Leedom is assigned to Thursday. The block of Graham and Koppel must occur on Sunday and Monday, or else Friday and Saturday. Either way, the block will fall on Sunday or Saturday, so one of those doctors must be the doctor assigned twice. Graham is only assigned once (Rule 2), so Koppel must be assigned twice, on Sunday and Saturday (Rule 1). Graham will then have to be assigned to either Monday or Friday (Rule 3). That leaves only Herrera or Nelson for Wednesday.

K	G/N/H	P	H/N	L	G/N/H	K
Su	Mo	Tu	We	Th	Fr	Sa

With Koppel on Sunday, **(D)** must be true and is thus the correct answer. The remaining answers all could be true, but need not be.

23. (E) Could Be True EXCEPT

The incorrect choices here will all be possible. The correct answer will be the exception—the one that must be false.

Using previous work is a huge time-saver on this question. Graham was assigned to Friday in the first sketch of the third question as well as the sketch for the fourth question. That eliminates **(A)**. Herrera can be assigned to Sunday in the first sketch for the third question, and can be assigned to Friday in the second sketch for the third question (and the fifth question, too). That eliminates **(B)** and **(C)**. And Koppel was assigned to Sunday in the sketches for both the fourth and fifth questions. That eliminates **(D)**. That leaves **(E)** as the correct answer. Leedom has never been assigned to Friday, and a little testing can prove why it is impossible.

If Leedom were assigned to Friday, the doctor assigned to Sunday and Saturday could only be Herrera, Koppel, or Nelson. If it were Herrera or Nelson, the other doctor couldn't be assigned to Monday (Rule 4) and would thus be assigned to Wednesday or Thursday. However, that doesn't leave two consecutive days for Graham and Koppel (Rule 3).

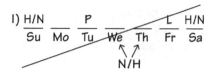

And if Koppel were assigned to Sunday and Saturday, Graham would have to be assigned to Monday. But that would leave Herrera and Nelson on Wednesday and Thursday, violating Rule 4.

II) K̶   G̶   P   H/N   N̶/H̶   L̶   K̶
   S̶u̶   M̶o̶   Tu   We   Th   Fr   Sa

Despite Leedom being a Floater, assigning Leedom to Friday creates an impossible scenario, thus confirming **(E)** as the correct answer.

Section III: Reading Comprehension

Passage 1: Recent Evidence about the Indus Valley Civilization

Q#	Question Type	Correct	Difficulty
1	Global	A	★
2	Detail (NOT)	C	★
3	Inference	E	★
4	Detail	B	★
5	Inference	C	★★
6	Inference	B	★★

Passage 2: Bordwell's Definition of Classical Era Films

Q#	Question Type	Correct	Difficulty
7	Global	E	★
8	Detail (EXCEPT)	D	★
9	Inference	B	★★
10	Global	A	★★★
11	Inference	D	★★★
12	Logic Reasoning (Parallel Reasoning)	E	★★★
13	Logic Reasoning (Weaken)	C	★★★

Passage 3: Blame in the Legal System

Q#	Question Type	Correct	Difficulty
14	Global	D	★★
15	Inference	A	★★
16	Inference	D	★★
17	Logic Reasoning (Point at Issue)	B	★★★
18	Logic Reasoning (Weaken)	E	★★
19	Logic Reasoning (Principle)	E	★★

Passage 4: Is The Big Bang a Unique Event?

Q#	Question Type	Correct	Difficulty
20	Global	A	★★★★
21	Inference	B	★★
22	Inference	D	★★★
23	Logic Function	C	★★★★
24	Logic Function	D	★★★
25	Global	E	★★
26	Inference	C	★★★★

Passage 1: Recent Evidence about the Indus Valley Civilization

Step 1: Read the Passage Strategically
Sample Roadmap

line #	Keyword/phrase	¶ Margin notes
1	major	
3	flourished	Indus Valley civ. details
10	long considered	
11	uninteresting; because	
12–14	but recent; without parallel	Recently found to be unique
16	masters	Urban design
21	suggesting	Democratic
23	also; apparently thrived	
24	for example	No army
28		Agriculture
29	In addition	Trade
35	causes; however	Why decline?
36–37	not certain; most contention; long-standing	Wheeler: massacre
41	But	
42	lack	
43	no	Auth: no evidence
44	In fact	
47	also shows	
50	most likely	
54	may	Relocation probably b/cof catastrophe
57	probably; Or	
58	may	

Discussion

The passage opens with a lot of dry details about the Indus Valley civilization: It flourished from 2600 B.C.E. to 900 B.C.E.; it was the largest ancient city, geographically; it contained 1,400 settlements; blah, blah, blah... It's all rather dull and extremely skimmable until the last sentence of the paragraph. The Contrast Keyword *but* introduces new evidence that changes the perception of this civilization from *uninteresting* to "*without parallel.*" That's a rather bold transition, and it sets up the rest of the passage. The **Topic** is the Indus Valley civilization. The **Scope** is the new findings from the recent excavations. And the **Purpose** is to inform readers of this new and exciting information. The rest of the passage is sure to provide all the glorious details.

And the second paragraph is quick to deliver. The Indus Valley cities had terraced brick homes and sewer systems. There was no major division of classes, which suggests a democratic government. And there were no weapons or armies. The third paragraph provides even more. The Indus Valley people were the first to cultivate rice and cotton. They were skilled agriculturists, and they developed a major trading system.

The last paragraph, *however*, introduces a greatly debated question: Why did such a civilization decline? The author introduces the common theory, proposed by archaeologist Mortimer Wheeler, that the Indus Valley people were wiped out by Indo-Aryan invaders. *But*, the author is quick to refute this theory by pointing to a lack of evidence. In fact, the author goes back to discussing the new excavations, which show no evidence of Indo-Aryans in the area at all. Instead, the evidence shows the civilization just moved to other areas, which is more likely the result of an environmental disaster (e.g., drought or earthquake). So, the civilization just got split up.

All together, the last three paragraphs deliver on the promise from the first paragraph, leading to the **Main Idea** that, based on new excavations, the Indus Valley civilization seems far more interesting than previously thought, and the civilization probably declined for environmental reasons, not because of invaders.

1. (A) Global

Step 2: Identify the Question Type
The question asks for the "main point of the passage," making this a Global question.

Step 3: Research the Relevant Text
As the question asks about the passage as a whole, the entire text is relevant. Don't go back into the details of the passage. Instead, consider the big picture, as predicted while reading the passage.

Step 4: Make a Prediction
The Main Idea is that new excavations show how the Indus Valley civilization is more interesting than originally thought and likely declined for environmental reasons, not because of invaders.

Step 5: Evaluate the Answer Choices
(A) is correct, perfectly summarizing the details revealed by the new excavations.

(B) is Out of Scope. While other Bronze Age civilizations are mentioned briefly at the beginning, the passage is overall focused exclusively on the Indus Valley civilization. Plus, this ignores all the new evidence from the recent excavations.

(C) is too narrow. This picks a couple of random details from the passage, but fails to mention the source of those details (the excavations) and how those details run counter to previous thoughts about the civilization.

(D) is a 180. The author uses the evidence from the recent excavations to draw several conclusions about the culture, any of which could be considered legitimate.

(E) is a Distortion. The author does not spend a lot of time complaining about how scholars were working with incomplete data. The passage is much more focused on how the recently discovered data provides new insight into the civilization.

2. (C) Detail (NOT)

Step 2: Identify the Question Type
The question asks for something "NOT cited in the passage." The reference to things cited makes this a Detail question. However, the correct answer will be the one detail that is *not* found.

Step 3: Research the Relevant Text
Unfortunately, the Indus Valley civilization is described throughout the entire passage, making all of the text relevant.

Step 4: Make a Prediction
There are too many details to predict which ones will be chosen for the wrong choices. And it would be practically impossible to predict the correct answer out of the countless details not mentioned in the passage. The only approach is to test the choices individually, making sure to eliminate the four choices that are mentioned directly by the author.

Step 5: Evaluate the Answer Choices
(C) is correct. There is no mention of the the people being nomadic. The only time the author mentions the Indus Valley people moving is in the last paragraph, and that's said to be due to environmental reasons, not nomadic behavior.

(A) is mentioned in lines 4–5.

(B) is mentioned in lines 26–27.

(D) is mentioned in lines 29–30.

(E) is mentioned in lines 8–9.

3. (E) Inference

Step 2: Identify the Question Type
The question asks for the "author's stance" on Wheeler's theory, as "[b]ased on the passage." That makes this an Inference question.

Step 3: Research the Relevant Text
Wheeler's theory is in the fourth paragraph, and the author's reaction to that theory begins on line 41.

Step 4: Make a Prediction
Wheeler's theory is about the cause of the civilization's decline. Wheeler claims the people were massacred by Indo-Aryans. *But*, the author is quick to dismiss that theory by pointing out the "lack of written evidence" (line 42) as well as the lack of "archaeological evidence" (lines 44–45). And the author goes on to show how the newly excavated evidence supports an alternative explanation: The civilization just moved and got split up (lines 49–53). The correct answer should point out the author's reasoned dismissal of Wheeler's theory.

Step 5: Evaluate the Answer Choices
(E) is correct. The author used the new evidence to reject Wheeler's theory, and the author is absolutely clear about it.

(A) is a 180. The author rejects the theory, so it would hardly be considered a worthy contribution to archaeology.

(B) is a 180. The author does not accept anything about the theory.

(C) is a Distortion. The disagreement comes across as rather forceful, not slight. And there's no indication that the author has any respect for the theory.

(D) is an Extreme Distortion. The author does reject the theory, but never goes so far as to say it was completely unworthy of any attention whatsoever. It was probably worth considering at one point, but now seems obsolete because of the newly found evidence.

4. (B) Detail

Step 2: Identify the Question Type
The question asks for something "cited in the passage," making this a Detail question.

Step 3: Research the Relevant Text
Wheeler's theory is in the last paragraph in lines 37–41. That's immediately followed by the Contrast Keyword [*b*]*ut*, which will provide the information that counters Wheeler's theory.

Step 4: Make a Prediction
Wheeler's theory is that the Indus Valley civilization's decline was caused by a massacre by Indo-Aryan invaders. However,

the author immediately counters that by citing "a lack of written evidence of such an event" and claiming "there is no archaeological evidence of battles" (lines 41–44).

Step 5: Evaluate the Answer Choices
(B) exactly matches what the author claims in opposition to Wheeler's theory.

(A) is a Faulty Use of Detail. The author mentions the area being seismically volatile in line 58. However, that's evidence to support a hypothetical alternative theory. It does not directly refute Wheeler's massacre theory.

(C) is a Faulty Use of Detail. The author does mention evidence of a drought in line 53, but that is only mentioned to suggest the plausibility of a different theory. It does not directly counter Wheeler's theory.

(D) is a Faulty Use of Detail. The lack of dominant rulers is mentioned in lines 19–20, but only as evidence of democracy. It has no bearing on Wheeler's massacre theory.

(E) is a Faulty Use of Detail. Agriculture is discussed in the third paragraph, but Wheeler's theory is about the civilization's decline, not its accomplishments.

5. (C) Inference

Step 2: Identify the Question Type
The question asks for something with which the author is "most likely to agree," making this an Inference question.

Step 3: Research the Relevant Text
There are no line or paragraph references, and the question doesn't ask about any content in particular. Thus, the entire passage is relevant.

Step 4: Make a Prediction
The correct answer could be based on any line or set of lines from anywhere within the passage. It's impossible to know exactly what the correct answer will focus on. So, test the choices individually. Eliminate choices that veer from the author's scope. And use clues in the answer choices to do research, as necessary.

Step 5: Evaluate the Answer Choices
(C) is correct. In the last paragraph, the author discusses possible theories why the civilization declined. In the last sentence (lines 57–60), the author mentions that the area was "seismically volatile" and that an earthquake may have caused people to flee the area. So, finding signs of such an earthquake could certainly help clarify why the civilization declined.

(A) is Extreme. The author merely says that a massive earthquake *may* have been responsible (lines 57–60). The author never says that's the *most likely* explanation.

(B) is Extreme. The author says an environmental catastrophe is the *most likely* explanation (lines 49–51). That doesn't mean it's the *only* possible explanation for the decline of the

Indus Valley civilization, let alone for that of other similar civilizations (which are outside the scope of this passage).

(D) is Out of Scope. There's no evidence that the people were unprepared for an earthquake, and the author makes no suggestion that they should have been better prepared for one.

(E) is Out of Scope. Such alteration of river courses would be caused by an earthquake (lines 57–59), which the author only says *may* have happened. The author does say that an environmental catastrophe is the most likely explanation (lines 49–51), but it doesn't have to be an earthquake.

6. (B) Inference

Step 2: Identify the Question Type
The question asks for something with which the author is "most likely to agree," making this an Inference question.

Step 3: Research the Relevant Text
The question asks about archaeological investigations into the Indus Valley civilization. That's discussed generally in the first paragraph, with the remaining paragraphs providing details gleaned from recent investigations.

Step 4: Make a Prediction
There are lots of details in the passage, so start by identifying the major themes. The first paragraph shows how the civilization was "long considered archaeologically uninteresting" but is now being seen as "without parallel"

thanks to recent investigations. The next two paragraphs provide evidence from those recent investigations. And the last paragraph shows how recent investigations counter at least one long-standing theory and provide evidence for alternate theories. Start with those ideas, and use clues in the answer choices to do research as necessary.

Step 5: Evaluate the Answer Choices
(B) is correct. This is supported by the first and last paragraph. In the first paragraph, it's only the recent research that has revealed evidence of the region's unique nature. And in the last paragraph, the recent research is responsible for countering a long-standing theory that now looks to be unreliable.

(A) is Out of Scope. There is no suggestion that any data was controlled by a small group of scholars.

(C) is Extreme. The Sumerian tablets mentioned in lines 32–34 do refer to the civilization, but there's no indication that those tablets contain the *only* written references.

(D) is an Extreme Distortion. The author never says that archaeologists have misinterpreted *most* data. In fact, the author never suggests any misinterpretation at all. It's just that the new data provides a more complete picture that was previously unknown.

(E) is Out of Scope. There is no suggestion of any recent trends in archaeology in general, nor is there any indication that archaeologists rely too much on written evidence.

Passage 2: Bordwell's Definition of Classical Era Films

Step 1: Read the Passage Strategically
Sample Roadmap

line #	Keyword/phrase	¶ Margin notes
3	defines	Bordwell: classical films have clear narrative; tell realistic story
13	anomalous	Musicals different
14–15	for example	
19	but	Ex: BB musical
21	Although	
22	not	
25	not to; but	Musical performance irrelevant to story
26	not	
27	but rather	
28	not; but	
32	?	Fits Bordwell's definiton?
33	no less	
36	argues	Bordwell: yes; theater set expectations
40	But	
41	does not	Auth: still not realistic
42	stretches	
43	problem exemplified	
45	not merely; but	
46	isn't	
47	but instead	
48	Even	
49	cannot	
50–51	too quickly dismisses	Bordwell too quick to generalize
52	not	
53	Because	
54	worthwhile	
55	first consider	
57	before	

Discussion

The passage starts by presenting the views of film scholar David Bordwell. Bordwell categorizes films of the classical era of Hollywood as straightforward narratives. They were made to tell a realistic story, and any technical elements were used solely for the sake of telling that story.

In the second paragraph, the author raises an anomaly from that time period: musicals. Musicals would actually interrupt the story just to have a musical performance. The author supports this with an extended example of a musical film by director Busby Berkeley. At the end of the paragraph, the author raises a question: Can musicals fit Bordwell's definition of the classical style?

In the third paragraph, Bordwell responds with a resounding "yes." Bordwell argues that, because musicals evolved from live theater, audiences recognize the conventions of musicals and thus accept them as "realistic." *But*, the author isn't convinced. The author claims that the musical performances do nothing to advance the story and are included just to show off artistic abilities—and even those who accept the film as a musical can recognize the break from the so-called "reality." The author concludes by saying that Bordwell is too quick to lump films into one genre, and scholars need to consider how audiences process what they're seeing before making such sweeping generalizations.

The **Topic** of the passage is Hollywood films of the classical era. The **Scope** is Bordwell's classification of those films and how musicals fit in. The author's **Purpose** is to criticize Bordwell's views. The **Main Idea** is that movie musicals offer an illustration of why Bordwell's definition of classical era films as realistic stories is inadequate.

7. (E) Global

Step 2: Identify the Question Type
The question asks for the "main point of the passage," making this a Global question.

Step 3: Research the Relevant Text
Because it asks about the entire passage, all of the text is relevant. Instead of going back into the text, consider the big picture that was predicted while reading strategically.

Step 4: Make a Prediction
The author's Main Idea is that Bordwell's definition of classical era films as realistic stories is inadequate, and movie musicals provide an example why it's inadequate.

Step 5: Evaluate the Answer Choices
(E) matches the prediction and is correct.

(A) is a 180. This suggests musicals justify Bordwell's definition of classical era films, which contradicts the author's point that Bordwell's definition is misguided.

(B) is a Distortion. Musicals might very well be chronological. What makes them unrealistic is that they just stop in the middle of the story so that people can show off their singing and dancing.

(C) is a 180. This is the point that Bordwell tries to make at the beginning of the third paragraph. However, the author refutes this claim and suggests Bordwell was too quick to generalize.

(D) is a Distortion. Musicals like those of Busby Berkeley surely do offer a challenge to Bordwell's definition. However, the author uses that to question Bordwell's classification, not to make any judgment about Berkeley's films. Perhaps Berkeley's films are good examples of the classical style, if there was a better definition than Bordwell's.

8. (D) Detail (EXCEPT)

Step 2: Identify the Question Type
Four of the answer choices will list something the "passage identifies," making this a Detail question. The EXCEPT indicates that the correct answer will be the one detail that is *not* mentioned in the passage.

Step 3: Research the Relevant Text
Bordwell's definition is presented in the first paragraph.

Step 4: Make a Prediction
There are a lot of details about Bordwell's definition in the first paragraph. There are countless details that are *not* mentioned, so predicting the correct answer will be nearly impossible. Instead, go through the details of the first paragraph and knock out choices that appear. The correct answer will be the one thing that is not mentioned or something that contradicts what Bordwell says.

Step 5: Evaluate the Answer Choices
(D) is correct. According to Bordwell's definition, the films are governed by "straightforward narratives" that "need to follow ... a chronological sequence of events." That does not include interludes.

(A) is mentioned in lines 11–12.

(B) is mentioned in line 5.

(C) is mentioned in lines 9–10.

(E) is mentioned in lines 5–6.

9. (B) Inference

Step 2: Identify the Question Type
The question asks for the way a term is defined throughout the passage. This is an Inference question variant that tests understanding of vocabulary in context.

Step 3: Research the Relevant Text
The term *realistic* is used throughout the passage, and often in quotes. If the definition of a repeated term is important, the author will likely define it early on, if not the very first time

it is used. The term first appears in line 10, so that's an ideal starting point.

Step 4: Make a Prediction
In lines 6–10, Bordwell argues that the elements of classical era films are designed to tell a realistic story, which is defined as one "in which the world of the story is self-sufficient and recognizably related to our own." This definition remains consistent throughout the rest of the passage, so the correct answer will mimic this idea.

Step 5: Evaluate the Answer Choices
(B) perfectly paraphrases the passage, touching on how the story exists in its own world and how it resembles our own world.

(A) is a Faulty Use of Detail. The narrative structure is mentioned in lines 3–6, but that's not what is said to make the films realistic.

(C) is a Distortion. This gets the logic backwards, suggesting that being realistic allows for the technical elements to tell a story. It's the other way around. The technical elements are designed to allow the story to be realistic.

(D) is a Faulty Use of Detail. The author mentions the audience in the last paragraph (lines 53–58). However, they judge the genre based on how they perceive and process the film, not necessarily on how realistic it is.

(E) is Out of Scope. The author never mentions films using a *variety* of narrative structures.

10. (A) Global

Step 2: Identify the Question Type
The question asks for the organization of the passage as a whole, making this a Global question.

Step 3: Research the Relevant Text
The question is more about structure than content, so use the margin notes to keep track of how the author moves from one idea to the next.

Step 4: Make a Prediction
In the first paragraph, the author introduces Bordwell's ideas. In the second paragraph, the author raises the anomalous example of musicals. In the third paragraph, the author describes Bordwell's reaction to musicals, then refutes Bordwell's views. The correct answer will follow this structure.

Step 5: Evaluate the Answer Choices
(A) matches the predicted structure, piece by piece.

(B) is a Distortion. The author does not take issue with Bordwell until the final paragraph.

(C) is a Distortion. The example in the second paragraph does not illustrate Bordwell's thesis. In fact, it seems to contradict his thesis.

(D) is a Distortion. The author does not take issue with Bordwell until the final paragraph.

(E) is Out of Scope. There is no research provided that supports Bordwell's thesis. And the author never acknowledges the legitimacy of Bordwell's response in the last paragraph. The author outright rejects it.

11. (D) Inference

Step 2: Identify the Question Type
The question asks for something with which the author is "most likely to agree," making this an Inference question.

Step 3: Research the Relevant Text
With no line references or Content Clues, the entire text is relevant.

Step 4: Make a Prediction
Except for the first paragraph, which is dominated by Bordwell's views, the correct answer could be supported by anything in the passage. Don't try to arbitrarily predict one particular idea. Instead, rely on the big picture and eliminate choices that are too strong or go outside the scope.

Step 5: Evaluate the Answer Choices
(D) is correct. This is supported in lines 53–58, in which the author argues that Bordwell should "consider how viewers process cinematic images and eventually come to accept them as conventions."

(A) is Extreme. Nothing indicates that breaking the narrative was *unique* to Berkeley's musicals. The author only mentions one Busby Berkeley musical, and that's just meant to be one example of such films.

(B) is a Distortion. In Bordwell's definition from the first paragraph, the technical elements were designed to tell a straightforward narrative. If anything, that suggests the *story* was simplistic, not the technical elements.

(C) is Extreme. According to lines 33–35, musicals, as well as comedies and melodrama, evolved from live theater. But that doesn't mean *all* classical era films were based on non-cinematic art forms.

(E) is a 180, at worst. The author discusses musicals in the second paragraph as an example of movies that routinely *break* from reality. And in the third paragraph, the author argues that those breaks are designed to be selfish expressions of artistic expertise (lines 42–48).

12. (E) Logic Reasoning (Parallel Reasoning)

Step 2: Identify the Question Type
The question asks for something "most closely parallel" to an idea expressed in the passage. That makes this a Parallel Reasoning question similar to those found in Logical Reasoning.

Step 3: Research the Relevant Text

The question asks for something parallel to the description of musical films of the 1930s, which are described in the second paragraph, along with an example of one by Busby Berkeley.

Step 4: Make a Prediction

In lines 14–16, the musicals are said to interrupt the narrative to present musical performances that are only loosely related to the plot. This is elaborated in lines 24–26, which say that such sequences don't contribute to the story; instead, they provide a break. The correct answer will transfer this quality to a novel, describing a novel that occasionally stops the story in order to go off on a tangent.

Step 5: Evaluate the Answer Choices

(E) is a match. Just how musicals will take a break from the story for a song-and-dance number, this describes how a book might take a break from its story to describe one character's fantasies.

(A) does not match. Musicals will take a break from the story. However, when the story is told, there's no indication that musicals leave out information needed to understand that story.

(B) does not match. Musicals are not said to focus on one character at a time until the end when all the characters meet.

(C) does not match. Musicals are not described as a collection of individual stories that form a complete picture by the end.

(D) is a 180. This describes a story that takes a break to provide relevant information. Musicals are said to take a break for performances that are *not* really relevant to the story.

13. (C) Logic Reasoning (Weaken)

Step 2: Identify the Question Type

The question asks for something that would "call [Bordwell's position] into question." That is standard wording for a Weaken question like those found in Logical Reasoning.

Step 3: Research the Relevant Text

The question refers to Bordwell's position in the first two sentences of the last paragraph. There, Bordwell claims that musicals are perceived as "realistic" because they are based on live theater, which has prepared the audience to expect the conventions of a musical.

Step 4: Make a Prediction

Live theater may prepare audiences who have seen those live shows. However, there's no evidence that people who attend movies are the same people who attend live theater. Bordwell assumes that the audiences for movie musicals have seen live theater. If they haven't, they wouldn't be prepared for the conventions of live theater, and Bordwell's argument would be ruined.

Step 5: Evaluate the Answer Choices

(C) is correct. As predicted, this suggests that there are movie audiences that did not attend live theater. And, because they perceived the movie the same way as people who *had* attended live theater, this suggests that live theater is irrelevant to people's expectations, contrary to Bordwell's claims.

(A) is irrelevant. What's true for reviewers is not necessarily true for general audiences. Besides, even if they liked the non-realistic scenes, Bordwell's point is that audiences expect such departures and thus still accept the structure as overall realistic.

(B) is irrelevant. It doesn't matter whether or not audiences enjoy the performances. The argument is about whether or not they perceive the film as realistic.

(D) is irrelevant. There is no connection between attention span and seeing the musicals as realistic.

(E) is a 180. If the movies have a similar style to live theater, that could only strengthen Bordwell's contention that live theater prepared moviegoers for what to expect.

Passage 3: Blame in the Legal System

Step 1: Read the Passage Strategically
Sample Roadmap

line #	Keyword/phrase	¶ Margin notes
Passage A		
4	But	Legal system assumes free will
6	For example	Author: exceptions exist
9	crucial; whether all	
11	whehter some	Are any acts free?
12	After all	
13	no	
15	suggests; no	Neuroscience suggests not
16	therefore	
17	One thing seems clear: if; does	
18	at best	if free will, it's minimal
19	small factor	
20	In fact	
21	so small	
24	should thus; removed	Author: remove blame from law
25	backward-looking	
26	impossible	
29	Instead	
30	has to	Look forward instead
Passage B		
33	paradox: if	Can blame be removed?
36	?	
40	deeply	Blame rooted in psyche
41–42	considerable doubt	Author: unlikely to remove
46	But	Tried rehab in past, public resisted
47	waned; backlash	
49	but	
50	unwilling	
51	useful	Author: blame serves social funtion
52	even if	
54	worthless	Criminal justice system should understand and keep blame
57	should also	

KAPLAN

Discussion

The author of passage A raises a challenge to the legal system. The legal system assumes that people always act freely, but the author contends that some actions are not deliberate, citing the example of people with neurological disorders.

Because of this, the author raises a *crucial* legal question in the second paragraph: Are all of our actions beyond our control, or do we have *some* free will? When such a question is raised, that usually helps confirms the author's **Topic** and **Scope**. In this case the Topic is free will, and the Scope is the question of how much free will we have and what that means for the legal system.

Neurologically, the author suggests that nothing in our brain is really "free," as every part of the brain is connected to some other part. And in the third paragraph, the author suggests that any free will we have, if it even exists, may be insignificant.

The Conclusion Keyword *thus* in the fourth paragraph reveals the author's **Purpose** and **Main Idea**. The author intends to persuade the reader, arguing that the legal system should abandon the concept of blame, as assigning blame requires untangling the complex questions of free will.

The author of passage B also addresses the role of blame in the legal system, raising the question of whether blame could be removed when it's so deeply entrenched within the system. Again, raising a question illustrates the author's **Topic** and **Scope**. In this case, the Topic is blame, and the Scope is the question of how to remove it from the legal system.

The second paragraph reveals why removing blame could be difficult. It's not just a legal issue, it's a psychological issue. The concept of blame is deeply rooted in the human psyche, which makes the author doubt the ability to remove it from the legal system.

In the third paragraph, the author even mentions unsuccessful attempts from the past. Instead of blaming criminals, the legal system once tried rehabilitating them. *But*, the public was unwilling to accept that choice was not a factor and that people could be changed.

In the final paragraph, the author argues that there must be some social benefit to blame, even if it's a false concept. The Opinion Keyword *should* (line 57) indicates the author's **Purpose** and **Main Idea**. This author also intends to persuade the reader. However, this author's point, as expressed in the final sentence, is that the legal system needs to respect the social need for blame and better understand why it's so important.

Before moving to the questions, it's important to consider the relationship between the passages. Both authors address the role of blame in the legal system. And both authors admit that blame may be a false concept, as behavior is biological and not necessarily made by choice. However, the author of passage A uses that to argue for the removal of blame from the legal system, while passage B argues for keeping blame in because it serves some social function.

14. (D) Global

Step 2: Identify the Question Type
The question asks what both authors are "primarily concerned" with overall, making this a Global question.

Step 3: Research the Relevant Text
As with any Global question, the entire text is relevant. Instead of going back into the passages, consider the big picture as predicted while reading strategically.

Step 4: Make a Prediction
The Main Idea of both passages centers around the role of blame in the legal system. The correct answer should address that concept.

Step 5: Evaluate the Answer Choices
(D) is correct, addressing the very question that both passages address in their conclusions.

(A) is Out of Scope for passage A. Rehabilitation and public support is only addressed in passage B (lines 45–50).

(B) is too narrow for passage A, and mostly Out of Scope for passage B. Brain science is really only addressed in the second paragraph of passage A, while passage B's discussion of the human psyche in its second paragraph is tangentially related to free will, at best.

(C) is Out of Scope for passage B. This assumption is only addressed at the very beginning of passage A.

(E) is a Distortion. Both authors may suggest these concepts are comparable. However, that's a minor point, at best, in service of the primary question about the role of blame in the legal system.

15. (A) Inference

Step 2: Identify the Question Type
The question asks for the "attitude of the author of passage B." The answer to an author's attitude question is never directly stated in the passage, but can be inferred by the author's language. That makes this an Inference question.

Step 3: Research the Relevant Text
The question asks how the author of passage B would react to the argument made in passage A. The main argument of passage A is made in the last paragraph, and the question that conclusion raises is addressed throughout passage B.

Step 4: Make a Prediction
The argument in passage A is that blame should be removed from the legal system (lines 24–25). The author of passage B

addresses that immediately by raising the question of whether it's possible. The author of passage B directly claims to have "considerable doubt" that it can be done (lines 41–43), even if the the author of passage B agrees with the author of passage A that blame may be a "false" concept (line 52). The correct answer will express the second author's doubt, despite agreeing with the theoretical idea.

Step 5: Evaluate the Answer Choices

(A) is correct, identifying the author's fundamental agreement while also addressing the stated doubt.

(B) is Out of Scope. The "intellectual acceptance" part holds up, but there's no discussion of the *fear* of consequences of widespread acceptance.

(C) is Extreme. The authors generally agree on a lot of the basic premises. And the author of passage B merely expresses some doubt. That hardly qualifies as "forceful rejection."

(D) is a Distortion. The author of passage B has a number of opinions on the concepts discussed. That does not indicate neutrality.

(E) is a Distortion. The author of passage B is sympathetic and does express doubt. However, the author of passage B only raises doubt about whether the other author's recommendation would work. There is no criticism of the theoretical logic behind the argument.

16. (D) Inference

Step 2: Identify the Question Type

The question asks for the meaning of a given phrase, which is a variation of Inference that tests vocabulary in context. However, instead of providing the meaning directly, the correct answer will be another term from elsewhere in the passage that conveys the same meaning.

Step 3: Research the Relevant Text

The question refers to the phrase "forward looking" in line 30. Start with that phrase and the surrounding lines for context. Then consider where the author of passage B discusses a similar concept.

Step 4: Make a Prediction

In lines 29–32, the author of passage A indicates that being "forward looking" involves considering how lawbreakers are "likely to behave in the future." The only time passage B mentions future behavior of lawbreakers is in the third paragraph, in which the legal system experimented with rehabilitating criminals. The correct answer will likely refer to a term in that paragraph.

Step 5: Evaluate the Answer Choices

(D) is correct, as it is the only choice that refers to something that looks at a lawbreaker's future actions.

(A) is a 180, as it refers to something that is already deeply rooted, not something that would occur in the future.

(B) does not match. This merely describes a type of argument. It does not reflect how a certain group of people will behave in the future.

(C) is a 180. This describes how people already think. It's not about looking forward at how people will act in the future.

(E) does not match. This describes a reaction to something that is already occurring. It does not indicate looking ahead to the future.

17. (B) Logic Reasoning (Point at Issue)

Step 2: Identify the Question Type

The question asks for something about which both authors *disagree*, making this a Point at Issue question such as those found in Logical Reasoning.

Step 3: Research the Relevant Text

As this question does not focus on any specific concept, the entire passages are relevant. Instead of going back into the content, consider the big picture of both passages.

Step 4: Make a Prediction

Both authors agree about the fundamental issue of blame as a faulty concept. However, the most prominent disagreement is in their main points. The author of passage A suggests that blame should be removed from the legal system, while the author of passage B says blame should be kept in because it serves some unknown social benefit. The correct answer will likely address the question of whether or not blame should be assigned in the legal system.

Step 5: Evaluate the Answer Choices

(B) is the correct answer, as it addresses the debated question of assigning blame in the legal system.

(A) is Out of Scope for passage B. The author of passage B only refers to criminal activity, not actions in general. Thus, the author of passage B offers no opinion on this matter. And as they relate to just criminal activity, both authors would *agree* that most choices are not made freely.

(C) is Out of Scope. Neither author addresses imprisonment.

(D) is Out of Scope. The author of passage A doesn't really get into actions that are "completely determined by physical processes." And the author of passage B doesn't address such actions at all.

(E) is a Distortion. The authors are arguing about removing blame from the legal system, not from everyday life. And only the author of passage B discusses how easy or difficult that might be.

18. (E) Logic Reasoning (Weaken)

Step 2: Identify the Question Type
The question asks for something that would "cast doubt" on the argument in passage B, making this a Weaken question like those found in Logical Reasoning.

Step 3: Research the Relevant Text
The author's argument is based on the entire passage, so the entire text of passage B is relevant. Instead of going back into the passage, consider the big picture.

Step 4: Make a Prediction
The conclusion of passage B comes in the final paragraph, where the author says that the legal system should keep using blame and should seek to better understand why people blame in the first place. However, the author only claims to *sense* some social benefit to blaming people (lines 51–52). That's not very convincing. That could be weakened by showing how blame is not important to society.

Step 5: Evaluate the Answer Choices
(E) is correct. While this doesn't go so far as to disprove the author's point, if some societies don't even have the concept of blame, that would question its usefulness.

(A) is irrelevant and a Faulty Use of Detail. This does nothing to address the use of blame in the legal system. If anything, it only refers to the neurological details from passage A, not passage B.

(B) is Out of Scope. How parts of the brain might become isolated has no effect on the argument about blame being assigned in the legal system.

(C) is Out of Scope. How people react to a repeated stimulus has nothing to do with the author's argument about blame.

(D) is irrelevant. It doesn't matter what some governments do. The author's argument is about what they *should* do, even if that's completely different than what those governments are doing now.

19. (E) Logic Reasoning (Principle)

Step 2: Identify the Question Type
The correct answer will "conform to the policy" advocated in passage A, but not the one from passage B. A policy is a general concept, and finding a specific circumstance that conforms to a general concept is the task of an Apply the Principle question, like those found in Logical Reasoning.

Step 3: Research the Relevant Text
The policies advocated in passages A and B are expressed in lines 24–25 and lines 55–59, respectively.

Step 4: Make a Prediction
The author of passage A pushes removing blame entirely from the legal system. The author of passage B advocates to keep blame in and work on better understanding it. The correct answer should describe a legal circumstance that does not invoke the concept of blame.

Step 5: Evaluate the Answer Choices
(E) is correct. This denies determining culpability (i.e., blame), which is consistent with the policy in passage A and contrary to the one in passage B. Further, the idea of considering the criminal's future behavior is also consistent with the policy from passage A.

(A) is Out of Scope. Neither policy addresses the concept of shame.

(B) is a 180. This suggests excluding people who are unwilling to assign blame. In other words, jurors must be willing to assign blame, which would contradict the policy in passage A.

(C) is Out of Scope. The policies are about assigning blame, not assessing one's state of mind.

(D) is a 180, at worst. The policy in passage A is based on neurological evidence. There is nothing to suggest that the author of passage A would want to be suspicious of such evidence.

Passage 4: Is The Big Bang a Unique Event?

Step 1: Read the Passage Strategically
Sample Roadmap

line #	Keyword/phrase	¶ Margin notes
1	posit	Big Bang theory
7	not; unique	C & C: Big Bang not unique
11	but not	Our universe is part of multiverse
15	initially	C & C studied time
21	Therefore	
23	For example	Entropy = disorder
27	So if	More time, more disorder
30	While	
32	mystery	Why did the universe start small/hot?
34	extremely unlikely	Unlikely
37	innovation; argue	C & C: cold, empty more likely
39	not	
41	Recent	G & V: energy fluctuations cause big bangs
49	On this view	
51	highly improbable	Author: C & C theory likely
52–53	not that unlikely; Indeed; likely not even; unique	

Discussion

The passage opens up with a quick description of the Big Bang theory (the actual physical theory, not the popular sitcom). To sum up: Our universe started out really small and hot, expanded a whole lot really quickly, and has since continued to get bigger and cool down.

The second paragraph introduces two physicists, Sean Carroll and Jennifer Chen, who argue that the Big Bang was just one of several similar events that happened regularly over an immensely extended period of time. According to Carroll and Chen, the Big Bang was just the beginning of *our* universe, which is part of a larger multiverse. This settles the **Topic** of the passage as our universe, with the **Scope** focused on the multiverse theory of Carroll and Chen. The rest of the passage provides details that support that theory, and that serves as the **Purpose** of the passage.

According to the third paragraph, Carroll and Chen started by studying time. What follows is a technical discussion of time, entropy, and the second law of thermodynamics and entropy. The author provides an example for clarification. In short, the second law of thermodynamics suggests that things get more disordered as time moves forward (i.e., more entropy).

In the fourth paragraph, the author claims that the Big Bang theory is consistent with the second law of thermodynamics. However, that raises the question: Why was our universe a small, hot, dense dot to begin with? It seems an unlikely starting point, and Carroll and Chan argue that a cold, large, empty space is a more likely starting point for everything—but that doesn't seem like the kind of environment that would experience a sudden expansion.

In the fifth paragraph, the author introduces two more physicists who claim that empty space can still have energy fluctuations, and those fluctuations can produce big bangs in various separate areas. Carroll and Chen use that information to support their view that our universe's Big Bang was one such fluctuation among a vast, considerably larger (and very disordered) multiverse.

In the last paragraph, the author expresses agreement. As a single event that started everything, the beginning of our universe seems unlikely. But as one of several similar events that occurred withing a vast multiverse, it actually seems pretty likely. That confirms the author's **Main Idea**: Carroll and Chen have developed a convincing theory that the beginning of our universe was just one of several similar events that occurred as part of a larger multiverse.

20. (A) Global

Step 2: Identify the Question Type
The question asks for the "main idea of the passage," which makes this a Global question.

Step 3: Research the Relevant Text
As with any Global question, the entire text is relevant. Don't go back into the details. Instead, focus on the big picture as predicted while reading the passage.

Step 4: Make a Prediction
The Main Idea of the passage is that Carroll and Chen have developed a theory that our universe's beginning was just one of several similar events as part of a much larger multiverse—a theory that the author endorses.

Step 5: Evaluate the Answer Choices
(A) is correct, providing a succinct summary of the supported theory.

(B) is too narrow. This focuses on a detail about entropy from the third paragraph, but completely misses the bigger picture about how that relates to our universe and its place in a larger multiverse.

(C) is a 180. Carroll and Chen do not dispute this view. They just argue that it wasn't the *only* occurrence of such an event.

(D) is too narrow. This point is suggested in the fourth paragraph, but that is just one minor point in service of the main point about how the beginning of our universe was not unique and is one of several similar instances within a larger multiverse.

(E) is a Faulty Use of Detail. Carroll and Chen are not merely interested in the existence of other universes. Their point is more about how our universe began (with the Big Bang) and the regular occurrence of other similar events. It's about the events that create universes, not the universes themselves.

21. (B) Inference

Step 2: Identify the Question Type
The question asks what a particular term *means*, which makes this an Inference question variant that asks for the definition of a term in context of the passage.

Step 3: Research the Relevant Text
The question points to the last sentence of the second paragraph. Be sure to consider the entire sentence and any relevant surrounding text, not just the term in question.

Step 4: Make a Prediction
The last sentence of the second paragraph (lines 9–14) describes how our universe is actually part of a larger multiverse, and that we will never see any of that multiverse that is outside our "cosmic bubble". So, that cosmic bubble is just the one area of the multiverse in which we live.

Step 5: Evaluate the Answer Choices
(B) is correct. The cosmic bubble is our universe, the one part of the larger multiverse that we can see.

(A) is a 180. The cosmic bubble is just our small part of that all-encompassing multiverse.

(C) is a Faulty Use of Detail. The cosmic bubble refers to where we are now, not what happened immediately after the Big Bang.

(D) is a 180. The cosmic bubble describes the actual physical universe we can observe, not some theoretical idea.

(E) is a Faulty Use of Detail. The author has not mentioned entropy by this point, and low entropy describes the beginning of our universe—not the current version in which we live.

22. (D) Inference

Step 2: Identify the Question Type
The question asks for the "author's stance," which is similar to asking for the author's attitude. An attitude is implied by the language of the passage rather than directly stated, making this an Inference question.

Step 3: Research the Relevant Text
The author remains fairly neutral until the very last paragraph. Use that paragraph for reference.

Step 4: Make a Prediction
In the last sentence of the last paragraph, the author claims the theory to be *likely*. It's certainly a favorable stance, if not a particularly forceful one. The correct answer should be generally positive, but not overly so.

Step 5: Evaluate the Answer Choices
(D) is correct. The author is mostly just reporting the details, but is sympathetic (i.e., expressing some agreement).

(A) is a 180. The author is supportive of the theory and says nothing adversarial about it.

(B) is a 180. The author is supportive, not dismissive.

(C) is a 180. The author shows no skepticism. In fact, the author claims the theory is likely.

(E) is Extreme. The author merely claims the theory is likely. That's far short of being a zealous proponent.

23. (C) Logic Function

Step 2: Identify the Question Type
This is an unusual question stem that works like a Logic Function question, but in reverse. Logic Function questions typically provide some detail from the passage and ask for its purpose. In this case, the question provides the purpose (the correct answer will support a given claim) and asks for the detail that serves that purpose.

Step 3: Research the Relevant Text
The claim in question is in lines 36–39. Start there, and use Keywords and the surrounding lines for context to find support for that claim.

Step 4: Make a Prediction
The claim in question is part of the fourth paragraph, which raises the mystery of why our universe would start so small and dense. This is a mystery because it goes against the random nature of the universe, as described in the previous paragraph. Carroll and Chen use those details from the third paragraph to support their innovative idea that everything actually started out in a large, cold, empty space, and the beginning of our universe was just one occurrence within that space. So, the correct answer should cite the third paragraph as the support for the claim in question.

Step 5: Evaluate the Answer Choices
(C) is correct.

(A) is incorrect. The first paragraph just describes the Big Bang that started our universe, but offers no support for the vast, empty space theory.

(B) is incorrect. The second paragraph presents the theory posited by Carroll and Chen, but no support is given for that theory or the claim in question until the third paragraph.

(D) gets the logic backwards. The details in the fourth paragraph support the ideas in the fifth paragraph, not the other way around.

(E) is incorrect. The sixth paragraph provides the author's opinion about the claims of Carroll and Chen, but does not provide any logical support.

24. (D) Logic Function

Step 2: Identify the Question Type
The phrase "primarily serves to" indicates a Logic Function question. The question is asking why the author mentions certain people in the fifth paragraph.

Step 3: Research the Relevant Text
The question stem directly refers to details from the fifth paragraph, but be sure to consult the margin notes to understand the context.

Step 4: Make a Prediction
The details provided by Garriga and Vilenkin help resolve the mystery posited in the previous paragraph. Then, Carroll and Chen use that information to further their own point of view. The correct answer will describe one or both of these purposes.

Step 5: Evaluate the Answer Choices
(D) is correct. Garriga and Vilenkin's claims address the mystery raised in the fourth paragraph, and provide support for how Carroll and Chen's theory resolve that mystery.

(A) is a 180, at worst. Garriga and Vilenkin actually suggest why big bangs would happen in the first place. They don't question any assumptions of the Big Bang theory.

(B) is a 180. The evidence from Garriga and Vilenkin support, not reject, the claims of Carroll and Chen.

(C) is a Distortion. The claims of Garriga and Vilenkin offer support for Carroll and Chen's theory, but do not illustrate any implications of that theory.

(E) is a 180, at worst. Their observations provide a basis for Carroll and Chen's theory. It's consistent with that theory, not an alternative.

25. (E) Global

Step 2: Identify the Question Type
The question asks for the "primary purpose" of the entire passage, making this a Global question.

Step 3: Research the Relevant Text
As with any Global question, the entire text is relevant. Instead of going back into the text, consider the purpose as predicted while reading the passage strategically.

Step 4: Make a Prediction
The author's purpose was identified as providing support for the theory posited by Carroll and Chen.

Step 5: Evaluate the Answer Choices
(E) is correct.

(A) is a Distortion. The only established principle in the passage is the Big Bang theory. Carroll and Chen don't raise any new consequences of that theory. They just offer a new view of how it might not be as unique as originally believed.

(B) is a Distortion. Carroll and Chen are merely expressing their own new ideas about the significance of the Big Bang theory. They are not challenging any particular view.

(C) is Out of Scope. There is no dispute to chronicle.

(D) is Out of Scope. There are no competing theories for the author to judge between. The Big Bang theory still stands, it's just that Carroll and Chen think it occurred for our universe, and perhaps others, within a multiverse.

26. (C) Inference

Step 2: Identify the Question Type
The question asks for something that "can be inferred," making this an Inference question.

Step 3: Research the Relevant Text
The question provides no line reference or Content Clue, so the entire text is relevant.

Step 4: Make a Prediction
As the correct answer could be based on any details from the passage, making a prediction will not be possible. Instead, go through the choices and use the big picture to eliminate choices that are outside the scope of the passage. Then, use the clues in the choices to research as necessary.

Step 5: Evaluate the Answer Choices
(C) is correct. This is directly supported in lines 31–34. The author says "[s]uch a low entropy universe," referring directly back to the previous sentence, which describes a "small, hot, and dense universe."

(A) is a 180. The suggestion is that the multiverse started as a vast, cold, and empty space. Big bangs occurred within that cold and empty space.

(B) is a 180. The initial state of the *larger multiverse* is assumed to be a cold, empty space. *Our* universe began with the Big Bang, as a small, hot, dense universe.

(D) is Out of Scope. Our universe is said to be part of one big multiverse, but the author never goes up another level to suggest that that multiverse is part of an even bigger series of multiverses.

(E) is a Distortion. The second law of thermodynamics provides a rule about time, but there's no indication that it was devised to answer any question in particular.

Section IV: Logical Reasoning

Q#	Question Type	Correct	Difficulty
1	Main Point	B	★
2	Point at Issue	E	★
3	Assumption (Sufficient)	D	★
4	Method of Argument	E	★
5	Parallel Reasoning	B	★
6	Role of a Statement	A	★★
7	Strengthen (EXCEPT)	B	★★
8	Principle (Identify/Inference)	A	★★
9	Flaw	E	★
10	Assumption (Necessary)	C	★★
11	Flaw	C	★★★
12	Strengthen	B	★
13	Assumption (Necessary)	E	★★
14	Role of a Statement	A	★★
15	Parallel Flaw	B	★
16	Flaw	E	★★★
17	Assumption (Necessary)	D	★★
18	Inference	C	★★★
19	Strengthen/Weaken (Evaluate the Argument)	D	★★★
20	Inference	C	★★★
21	Main Point	E	★★
22	Weaken	D	★★★
23	Paradox	E	★★★★
24	Flaw	D	★★★★
25	Strengthen	C	★★

1. (B) Main Point

Step 1: Identify the Question Type
The question asks for the "conclusion drawn" in the argument, making this a Main Point question.

Step 2: Untangle the Stimulus
The researcher first presents what is "widely believed." That is somebody else's opinion, and the researcher is likely to dispute that. Sure enough, the Contrast Keyword [*b*]*ut* indicates the researcher's rebuttal: The belief is mistaken. What follows are geographic and meteorological facts that act as evidence for the researcher's rebuttal.

Step 3: Make a Prediction
The researcher's conclusion is a rebuttal of the widely held belief. For context, that view is that the Gulf Stream is responsible for England's mild winters. So, the correct answer will express how that view is mistaken.

Step 4: Evaluate the Answer Choices
(B) matches the prediction and is correct.

(A) is a Faulty Use of Detail. This restates the opposing view, which the researcher goes on to refute.

(C) is a Faulty Use of Detail. This is given as something *true*, which makes it a fact. And the facts are used as evidence to support the conclusion.

(D) is a Faulty Use of Detail. This is a fact given as evidence to support the researcher's conclusion.

(E) is a Faulty Use of Detail. Even though this is the last sentence of the stimulus, it is still just another fact given as evidence to support the conclusion.

2. (E) Point at Issue

Step 1: Identify the Question Type
The stimulus has two speakers, and the question asks for something they "disagree over," making this a Point at Issue question.

Step 2: Untangle the Stimulus
Edgar argues that nurses should be allowed to anesthetize patients without a doctor present because it's become a remarkably safe procedure. Janet counters this by saying that, despite the training nurses have, only doctors have the broader training needed should an emergency arise.

Step 3: Make a Prediction
Janet is implying that, in case of emergency, a doctor should still be present when anesthesia is administered. This goes against Edgar, who feels that a doctor is no longer needed. The correct answer will address this disagreement over the need for a doctor in the room.

Step 4: Evaluate the Answer Choices
(E) is correct. Edgar would say: No, nurse anesthetists don't always need doctor supervision. Janet would say: Yes, they do

always need doctor supervision, in case of emergency. And that's the source of disagreement.

(A) is a Distortion. They are not disputing whether nurses should administer anesthesia at all. They're both fine with that. The dispute is whether or not a doctor needs to be present.

(B) is Out of Scope for Edgar. Only Janet mentions the rarity of emergencies. Edgar has no opinion on the matter, stated or implied, so there's no reason to suggest he would disagree.

(C) is Out of Scope. Both speakers mention that nurses can be trained (and excellently so, according to Janet). However, neither one suggests a need for more training.

(D) is Out of Scope for Janet. Only Edgar mentions the increased safety of anesthesia. Janet does not refute that and only worries about emergencies, which she even admits are rare.

3. (D) Assumption (Sufficient)

Step 1: Identify the Question Type
The question asks for something *assumed* that would ensure the conclusion "follows logically," making this a Sufficient Assumption question.

Step 2: Untangle the Stimulus
The consumer is addressing a new law that would require removing logos from and adding warnings and disturbing pictures to cigarette packages. The consumer concludes that this will not affect the habits of regular smokers. The evidence is that regular smokers don't often look at the package when they take out a cigarette.

Step 3: Make a Prediction
The consumer only says that smokers don't usually look at the package when taking out a cigarette. But what about those few times that they do or other times they look at the packaging when not taking out a cigarette? What about when they go to buy the cigarettes or when they see ads for the cigarettes? The consumer fails to consider that, assuming that smokers would only be affected by seeing the package frequently when taking out a cigarette. If they don't see the package a lot, the packaging won't affect them.

Step 4: Evaluate the Answer Choices
(D) matches the prediction, and is correct.

(A) is Out of Scope. The legislation described has already been implemented, and the consumer claims it *won't* affect the habits of regular smokers. There is no suggestion about implementing other regulations that *would* affect regular smokers.

(B) is a Distortion. Even if this were true, the consumer claims that regular smokers will *not* look at the pictures frequently. So, it doesn't matter what would happen if they *did*.

(C) is a Distortion. This might support the consumer's point by showing why regular smokers would be unaffected even if they *did* see the warnings. However, what about the disturbing images? The consumer's argument is still incomplete because nothing guarantees that even a rare glimpse of those images wouldn't affect the habits of regular smokers.

(E) is Out of Scope. This might explain why regular smokers would be unaffected by removing the logos. However, there would still be warnings and disturbing pictures that could affect smokers' habits. The argument is still incomplete.

4. (E) Method of Argument

Step 1: Identify the Question Type
The word *by* indicates that the question is asking *how* Young responds to Warner. That makes this a Method of Argument question.

Step 2: Untangle the Stimulus
Warner makes an observation that competitive swimmers used to be mostly high school and university students, but now there are more swimmers competing after they graduate. Warner then argues that this is because swimmers now have better training regimens that allow for longer swimming careers. Young has a different explanation. While it used to be that swimmers had to stop competing so they could get a job, it's now possible for swimming to *be* their job. That's why they're competing longer.

Step 3: Make a Prediction
Warner had one explanation for longer swimming careers, but Young stepped in with an alternate explanation. The correct answer will describe Young's technique of providing an alternate view.

Step 4: Evaluate the Answer Choices
(E) is correct. Young offers an alternative explanation for why swimmers are competing longer.

(A) is a Distortion. Warner uses evidence of longer swimming careers to reach a conclusion that swimmers have better training regimens. Young never claims Warner's evidence weakens Warner's conclusion. Young just comes up with an alternative conclusion based on additional evidence.

(B) is a Distortion. The evidence for Warner's conclusion is that swimmers are having longer careers. Young doesn't weaken that evidence. In fact, Young accepts that evidence and instead draws a different conclusion.

(C) is a Distortion. Warner may be arguing that better training regimens are sufficient to bring about longer swimming careers. However, Young never addresses training regimens or implies that they are necessary. Instead, Young raises an entirely new explanation.

(D) is Out of Scope. This suggests that Young is accusing Warner of circular reasoning. That is not accurate. Young never directly attacks Warner's argument. Instead, Young merely raises an unconsidered alternative.

5. (B) Parallel Reasoning

Step 1: Identify the Question Type
The question asks for an argument "most similar in its reasoning" to the argument in the stimulus. That makes this a Parallel Reasoning question.

Step 2: Untangle the Stimulus
The businessperson concludes that Chen should be hired instead of Brenner. The evidence is that, although they are the only viable candidates, Brenner has a history of problems with coworkers.

Step 3: Make a Prediction
The structure here is relatively straightforward. Two options are presented. One is said to have a problem, so the businessperson argues for choosing the other option. The correct answer will follow this structure.

Step 4: Evaluate the Answer Choices
(B) is correct. Two options are presented (Mexico or Peru). One has a problem (Peru has floods), so the author argues for the other option (go to Mexico).

(A) does not match. Two options are presented, but this argument never chooses one over the other. Instead, it simply discourages delaying the selection, and it also leaves open the possibility of selecting both.

(C) does not match. This presents two options, but it puts the decision back on the decision-maker rather than arguing for one over the other.

(D) does not match. This presents two options. However, instead of choosing one over the other, this argument says to choose both.

(E) does not match. This presents two options. However, instead of eliminating one because of a problem, it supports choosing one because of a benefit. Furthermore, unlike the original argument, this one suggests that, eventually, both options can be selected.

6. (A) Role of a Statement

Step 1: Identify the Question Type
This question presents a claim from the stimulus and asks for the role it plays in the argument, making this a Role of a Statement question.

Step 2: Untangle the Stimulus
The psychologist starts by arguing that thinking can occur without language. What follows is evidence in the form of research. Infants were shown pictures of faces and were able to spot anomalies (e.g., faces with three eyes) even without

having language skills. Based on this, it is concluded that infants have thoughts of a typical face in their minds.

Step 3: Make a Prediction

The claim in question (a thought about the human face exists in infants' minds) is mentioned at the very end, preceded by the Conclusion Keyword [*t*]*hus*. That indicates it is a conclusion. However, it is a conclusion drawn by the research. The research, including that conclusion, is used to support the broader conclusion expressed in the first sentence: "Thinking can occur without language." So, the claim in question is certainly a conclusion, but it is a subsidiary conclusion that serves as evidence for the psychologist's main conclusion.

Step 4: Evaluate the Answer Choices

(A) matches the prediction and is correct.

(B) is a Distortion. The psychologist draws this conclusion based on the researchers' data. However, it is not directly attributed to the researchers, and it is not said to be the main conclusion of their research. It is just the conclusion the psychologist uses to support a broader point about thinking.

(C) is not accurate. The main point is the first sentence. The claim in question is a subsidiary conclusion that supports the main point.

(D) is a Distortion. The psychologist does not refute the fact that infants have no knowledge of language. In fact, the psychologist accepts that fact and is arguing that infants have thoughts even without that knowledge of language.

(E) is a Distortion. The hypothesis is the psychologist's conclusion in the first sentence. The claim in question is an example that supports the hypothesis. It is not itself a hypothesis in need of explanation.

7. (B) Strengthen (EXCEPT)

Step 1: Identify the Question Type

The question asks for information that would "support the [given] view," making this a Strengthen question. The EXCEPT indicates that four choices will actually strengthen the argument. The correct answer will be the one that doesn't—it will either weaken the argument or be irrelevant.

Step 2: Untangle the Stimulus

The nutritionist argues that osteoporosis (a bone disease) can be prevented by eating lots of fruits and vegetables and less meats and dairy, not by getting a lot of calcium (as is often believed). The nutritionist also argues that weight-bearing exercise (e.g., walking) also helps because resistance helps thicken bones.

Step 3: Make a Prediction

The nutritionist makes a lot of points but provides just one clear piece of evidence (bones get thicker from resistance during exercise). The argument lacks any evidence why fruits

and vegetables are good for bones, why meats and dairy are not, and why calcium isn't as important as is typically believed. To strengthen these claims, the nutritionist needs evidence. Four answers will provide supportive evidence. The correct answer will be irrelevant or will contradict at least one of the nutritionist's claims.

Step 4: Evaluate the Answer Choices

(B) is correct. This offers an entirely different way to help with osteoporosis (medical therapies) that has nothing to do with any of the nutritionist's recommendations. Therefore, it offers no support for any of the nutritionist's claims.

(A) does provide support. This helps confirm the nutritionist's evidence about weight-bearing exercise. If bone density decreased when people are weightless, that suggests weight is important to maintain (or increase) bone density.

(C) does provide support. This provides a link showing how low protein (i.e., less meat) relates to less osteoporosis.

(D) does provide support. This provides evidence that calcium does not necessarily help, as the nutritionist claims.

(E) does provide support. This provides a link showing how a high-vegetable, low-meat diet relates to less osteoporosis.

8. (A) Principle (Identify/Inference)

Step 1: Identify the Question Type

The correct answer will be a principle, making this an Identify the Principle question. While most such questions ask for principles that are consistent with the given information, this question asks for a principle "most at odds" with what's given. As there's no indication of an argument, this works more like an Inference question, and one that would ask for something contradictory or false.

Step 2: Untangle the Stimulus

A farm wants to test its cattle for a certain disease. Testing for this disease is required by other countries to which the farm wants to export beef. The government, however, won't allow the testing. The government's reasoning is that there's no scientific justification for the testing, and running the tests might scare the public into thinking there *was* scientific justification.

Step 3: Make a Prediction

The question asks for something with which the government's decision is most at odds. Because the government's decision is to prohibit testing the cattle, that would be at odds with any principle that, based on the information provided, suggests testing the cattle is warranted or prohibiting the testing is unwarranted. It may be difficult predicting a particular principle. Instead, look for an answer choice that provides a reason why, according to the given information, testing *should* be done or that the government has no grounds for prohibiting it.

Step 4: Evaluate the Answer Choices

(A) is correct. This suggests that the government has no right to prohibit testing that could help protect people, even if the government feels it's not justified. The desire to prohibit testing certainly goes against this principle.

(B) is a 180. This asks governments to determine whether testing is justified by the risk posed. The government in question has done that and has determined it's not justified. The government has then presented its opinion to the farm, which is consistent with this principle.

(C) is Extreme and a 180, at worst. The government never said the testing is *unnecessary*. The risk just isn't great enough to justify the testing. Besides, even if the government did consider the testing unnecessary, this principle is exactly what the government is doing. It would be acting on this principle, not at odds with it.

(D) is Out of Scope and a 180, at worst. There is no indication that taxpayer money would be used to perform the testing. And even if it were, this would justify the government's decision to prohibit testing because it finds the testing unwarranted.

(E) is Out of Scope. There is no indication that Quartzbrook's government requires anything of foreign companies. The government's decision is only about what the farm can and cannot do. If **(E)** is in reference to what is required by the countries Quartzbrook wants to export the beef, then that is also Out of Scope because the question stem is looking for something at odds with the Quartzbrook's government's prohibition on testing.

9. (E) Flaw

Step 1: Identify the Question Type

The question asks why the given argument is "vulnerable to criticism." That's a common indicator of a Flaw question.

Step 2: Untangle the Stimulus

The manager concludes ([*t*]*herefore*) that, to reduce exhaustion as much as possible, office workers should take several short vacations each year instead of just one or two long vacations. The evidence is that exhaustion is reduced after every vacation.

Step 3: Make a Prediction

First off, if the manager feels that vacations reduce exhaustion, that manager has never been on vacation with two kids. However, that's the evidence, which must be accepted for the sake of this question. The conclusion is suggesting that more vacations mean less exhaustion because each vacation reduces exhaustion. However, that assumes all vacations are equally beneficial. So, if each vacation reduced exhaustion by the same amount, then sure—more vacations mean less exhaustion. However, if long vacations were far more effective at reducing exhaustion,

then one long vacation might be better than three or four short ones. The manager overlooks that possibility, and the correct answer will address that.

Step 4: Evaluate the Answer Choices

(E) matches the prediction and is correct.

(A) is a Distortion. This only applies to short vacations. It's not a problem if the manager assumes that all short vacations are of equal value. The flaw is in assuming that *all* vacations, regardless of size, provide equal benefit.

(B) is Out of Scope. The manager is not arguing that this is the best solution for reducing exhaustion. The manager is merely arguing that many short vacations are better than a few long ones. That could still hold true, regardless of other possible solutions.

(C) is a Distortion. The argument is only about whether or not exhaustion is reduced. How one employee compares to the next is irrelevant.

(D) is a Distortion. This suggests that there might be an even more effective solution to reducing exhaustion: increasing the total number of vacation days. However, that doesn't have any effect on the manager's argument. It's still possible that many short vacations are better than a few long ones, even if there are other factors to consider.

10. (C) Assumption (Necessary)

Step 1: Identify the Question Type

The question asks for an "assumption required by the argument," making this a Necessary Assumption question.

Step 2: Untangle the Stimulus

Some people say that Neanderthals couldn't think symbolically. *However*, the author refutes that, suggesting that Neanderthals could, in fact, think symbolically. The evidence is that researchers determined a particular cave painting was made by a Neanderthal.

Step 3: Make a Prediction

This argument is based on Mismatched Concepts. The evidence of making a cave painting is used to support a conclusion about symbolic thinking. The author assumes these ideas are connected—that making cave paintings is indicative of thinking symbolically.

Step 4: Evaluate the Answer Choices

(C) is correct, making the necessary link between the cave paintings and symbolic thinking.

(A) is Out of Scope. The argument is not about manual dexterity. Whether we know they had such dexterity or not, this offers no connection to the concept of symbolic thinking.

(B) is Extreme. Neanderthals don't have to be the only hominids to have existed in *all* of Europe at the time. They just needed to be the ones in Spain who were responsible for the cave paintings. And that could still be true even if other hominids existed in Europe. If this answer had said that no other hominids lived in that cave in Spain 40,800 years ago, then it would have been another necessary assumption, just like **(C)**.

(D) is Extreme. The evidence provided doesn't have to be the very first piece of evidence to make such a suggestion. Even if there have been many other pieces of circumstantial evidence, that doesn't affect the argument.

(E) is a Distortion. The author is suggesting that people who *did* paint caves *were* able to think symbolically. The author is not assuming or implying anything about people who *can't* paint caves.

11. (C) Flaw

Step 1: Identify the Question Type
The question asks why the "argument is flawed," making this a Flaw question.

Step 2: Untangle the Stimulus
The conclusion ([*s*]*o*) is that Mary's application, if sent by regular mail, would be considered only if she mails it ten days before the deadline. The evidence is that regular mail takes up to ten days to reach the application's destination.

Step 3: Make a Prediction
The evidence says that regular mail takes *up to* ten days. That doesn't mean will it definitely take ten days. Maybe it will take just one or two. So, the author's use of the phrase "only if" is too strong. Mary doesn't *have* to send the application ten days early. She could wait a few more days and still be on time if the mail arrives early. She's risking that it will arrive late by doing so, but it's not guaranteed to arrive late if she sends it for example seven days before the due date. The correct answer will address this overlooked possibility.

Step 4: Evaluate the Answer Choices
(C) is correct. The author only considers the maximum of ten days and doesn't consider the minimum. Perhaps the mail can be delivered in less time, and Mary isn't obligated to send it out so early (even though she runs the risk of it being late if she does).

(A) is Out of Scope. The argument is based on what would happen *if* she were to apply and mail the application from Greendale. There's no need for this event to be established to draw a hypothetical conclusion.

(B) is Out of Scope. The argument is only about what would happen if she used regular mail. It doesn't matter what would happen if she decided to use express mail instead.

(D) is Out of Scope. The argument is not designed to determine whether or not Mary will qualify for the grant. It's only meant to determine whether or not her application will arrive in time to be considered. Timely receipt is considered necessary; the author never treats it as sufficient.

(E) is Out of Scope. The argument is based on the hypothetical situation of using regular mail. There's no need to consider what other methods, if any, are needed to guarantee timely delivery.

12. (B) Strengthen

Step 1: Identify the Question Type
The question asks for "additional evidence in support of [a] hypothesis," making this a Strengthen question.

Step 2: Untangle the Stimulus
The hypothesis (as stated in the question stem and in the last sentence) is that the Amazon River once flowed into the Pacific Ocean. The evidence is that the Amazon is now cut off from the Pacific Ocean by the Andes Mountains, yet there are fish in the river that are descended from now-extinct fish that only lived in the Pacific Ocean.

Step 3: Make a Prediction
If the ancestors of the fish only lived in the Pacific Ocean, then that is almost certainly where the ancestors came from. However, there's still the problem of the Andes Mountains being in the way. Unless those ancient fish had some unheard of mountain-climbing skills, they would have needed some other way to get from the Pacific Ocean to the Amazon. The author does offer a great hint by saying that the Amazon is *now* cut off from the Pacific by the Andes. That suggests there was a time when the Andes were *not* in the way. If the fish were alive back then, then they could have taken that direct route before the Andes formed. And that would provide the support the author needs.

Step 4: Evaluate the Answer Choices
(B) is correct. If the fossils predate the Andes, that suggests the fish were alive before the Andes formed, which makes it likely they had access to the hypothesized route between the Amazon and the Pacific.

(A) is a 180. This suggests that the fish in the Amazon may *not* be related to the ancient Pacific Ocean fish. That ruins the connection between the Amazon and the Pacific.

(C) is Out of Scope. Even if this were true, the evidence claims that the ancestor fish in question did *not* inhabit the Atlantic.

(D) is Out of Scope. It doesn't matter how long the Andes are. The fact remains that they cut the Amazon off from the Pacific, which offers no support for a one-time link between those two bodies of water.

(E) is a 180, at worst. This just suggests that the ancient ancestors, which inhabited the salty Pacific Ocean, were unlikely to survive in the fresh water of the Amazon River. So, there's no reason to believe the two bodies of water were linked.

13. (E) Assumption (Necessary)

Step 1: Identify the Question Type
The question asks for an "assumption required" by the argument, making this a Necessary Assumption question.

Step 2: Untangle the Stimulus
The columnist claims that banning performance-enhancing drugs (PEDs) will not stop their use. They provide too much of an advantage, and athletes will always try to get whatever advantage they can. *So*, the columnist concludes that PEDs should be allowed, but only in safe doses under the care of a doctor. In that manner, the risk is removed.

Step 3: Make a Prediction
In the first couple of sentences, the columnist is suggesting that athletes will ignore a ban on PEDs because they will do anything to gain an advantage. Thus, the ban would be futile and the risk wouldn't go away. And that's where the columnist's recommendation comes in. The columnist is assuming that allowing athletes to take doses in safe, controlled amounts will satisfy their need for an advantage. Then, they'd get the advantage they want in a safe way without exposing themselves to risk.

Step 4: Evaluate the Answer Choices
(E) is correct. If unsafe levels of PEDs provide no added advantage, then athletes could get all the advantage they desire from the safe levels recommended by the columnist. And the Denial Test shows why this assumption is necessary. If unsafe levels *did* create a major advantage over safe levels, then athletes would probably ignore the doctor's recommendation and go for unsafe levels because "top athletes will do whatever it takes to gain a big competitive advantage." The columnist can't have that happen.

(A) is Out of Scope. The argument makes no implication about the need for having the spectators' respect.

(B) is an Irrelevant Comparison. It doesn't matter whether or not some athletes get more benefit than others. As long as the athletes are okay with the safe doses, then the columnist's argument stands.

(C) is Out of Scope. It doesn't matter whether or not athletes think PEDs will help in cases when they don't actually help. It's still possible that safe doses would pose no risk.

(D) is Out of Scope. Whether or not doctors are willing to help now has no bearing on what would happen in the future if PEDs were recommended in measured doses. Perhaps doctors will change their mind, because then they could help prevent the athletes from the risks of overdosing.

14. (A) Role of a Statement

Step 1: Identify the Question Type
The question provides a claim and asks for the role it plays in the stimulus, making this a Role of a Statement question.

Step 2: Untangle the Stimulus
Max argues that, because technology is steadily destroying the environment, it is inevitable that humans will have to revert to a natural way of living. Cora argues that living with environment-changing technology *is* natural, and thus Max's point is unconvincing.

Step 3: Make a Prediction
The claim in question (it's natural for humans to use technology that changes the environment) is Cora's evidence to counter Max's argument. By claiming humans have to return to a "natural way of living," Max is implying that the current state of things (humans using technology to change the environment) is not natural. Cora's claim is meant to suggest that this implication is invalid.

Step 4: Evaluate the Answer Choices
(A) is correct. Max allegedly blames the terrible changes on technology, and the claim in question does suggest that using technology is natural (i.e., cannot be described as unnatural).

(B) is a Out of Scope. Cora only says that the use of technology is natural. There is no indication of any benefits.

(C) is a Distortion. Max's conclusion is about the need for humans to revert to nature, not about technology changing the environment. Further, Cora does not dispute Max's claim about technology changing the environment. She just claims it's more natural than Max implies.

(D) is a 180, at worst. Cora doesn't think it will be difficult to revert to a natural way of living. On the contrary, Cora's claim suggests that humans are *already* living naturally.

(E) is Out of Scope. Neither Max nor Cora address the concept of morality.

15. (B) Parallel Flaw

Step 1: Identify the Question Type
The correct answer will exhibit "flawed reasoning" that is "most similar to the flawed reasoning" in the stimulus. That makes this a Parallel Flaw question.

Step 2: Untangle the Stimulus
The commentator is trying to argue that childhood obesity is not a problem. The evidence is that the average weight of children has barely changed in eight years (only 1 pound greater). Because of that, the commentator concludes (*so*) that the percentage of obese children can't have changed much.

Step 3: Make a Prediction
The average weight is a middle ground between the heaviest kids and lightest kids. The commentator is assuming that a similar average means that children's weights are spread out about the same. However, it's possible that the proportion of obese kids has, actually, increased dramatically. There just

might also be a lot more highly underweight kids that balance out the average. The commentator fails to consider the possibility of a counterbalance. The correct answer will commit the same flaw of only looking at the average without considering how the extremes balance out.

Step 4: Evaluate the Answer Choices
(B) is correct. Like the original argument, this one only focuses on the average. And like the original, this one fails to consider the counterbalance. It's possible that the proportion of very highly paid employees has, in fact, increased, but that's been counterbalanced by more employees making very low salaries.

(A) does not match. This argument makes a conclusion about averages based on people's beliefs. This confuses beliefs with facts, but that's not the flaw in the original argument.

(C) does not match. This argument does contain an overlooked possibility (a lot of new office buildings could have been built, too), but it's not based on the misuse of average figures.

(D) does not match. This is flawed in that it makes an unwarranted scope shift from the amount of calories in meals to people's weight. However, it's not the same as the original argument, which is based on averages and proportions *not* changing.

(E) does not match. This tries to tempt those who notice the same time frame of eight years. However, this argument suggests that an average (house price) has increased because a proportion (spending on housing) has increased. This is not the same as arguing that a proportion is *not* increasing because the average is not increasing much.

16. (E) Flaw

Step 1: Identify the Question Type
The question asks why the given "argument is flawed," making this a Flaw question.

Step 2: Untangle the Stimulus
The editorial is about a book by Kramer, which contends that coal companies are responsible for economic difficulties. The conclusion ([t]*hus*) is that this contention is false—that coal companies are not, in fact, responsible. The evidence is that Kramer's support is unconvincing. Kramer's support comes from coal employees who complain that coal companies don't invest in other industries. However, the editorial provides counterevidence showing that coal companies *do* invest in other industries.

Step 3: Make a Prediction
The editorial does a great job of disputing Kramer's evidence. However, that doesn't mean Kramer's conclusion is wrong, as the editorial argues. It's possible that coal companies *are* responsible for the economic difficulties, just not for the

reasons Kramer provides. Bad evidence is not the same as a bad conclusion. The correct answer will expose this commonly tested flaw.

Step 4: Evaluate the Answer Choices
(E) matches the prediction, and is correct.

(A) is Out of Scope. The editorial does argue that coal companies are not to blame, but it is not blaming anybody else.

(B) is Out of Scope. The editorial doesn't show any concern for ruining the coal industry's reputation. The editorial is only concerned about the accuracy of the information provided.

(C) a Distortion. It is said that the coal employees are disgruntled, which may suggest they have ulterior motives. However, that is not what the editorial argues. The editorial questions the accuracy of the employees' claims, not the motives behind them.

(D) is Out of Scope. This describes the flaw of confusing necessary and sufficient conditions, which is based on misusing Formal Logic. However, there is no Formal Logic to be found, and nothing is presented as or implied to be sufficient or necessary.

17. (D) Assumption (Necessary)

Step 1: Identify the Question Type
The question asks for an "assumption required by the argument," making this a Necessary Assumption question.

Step 2: Untangle the Stimulus
The conclusion is that health-care facilities have to require mandatory influenza vaccines for their employees. The evidence is that the vaccines can reduce the spread of harmful viruses, and health-care facilities have a duty to protect patients from harm.

Step 3: Make a Prediction
If the vaccines help prevent harm to patients, then they would certainly help health-care facilities fulfill their duty. However, to achieve this, do facilities really have to take the extreme route of setting up mandatory vaccination policies? Couldn't they just offer free vaccinations or provide employees with incentives? The author assumes that there is no other solution and that mandatory vaccination is the only way to ensure compliance.

Step 4: Evaluate the Answer Choices
(D) is correct, suggesting that another policy (voluntary vaccination) wouldn't help. The Denial Test confirms this. What if voluntary vaccination *could* adequately protect patients? In that case, there would be no need to make vaccination mandatory. That would ruin the author's argument, so the author must assume voluntary vaccination won't work.

(A) is Out of Scope. Even if the employees did see mandatory vaccination policies as a rights violation, that's an entirely different argument. This argument is only concerned with health-care facilities fulfilling their duty to protect patients.

(B) is Extreme. Influenza viruses don't have to be the *most* harmful. As long as they're harmful at all, they should be dealt with to prevent any patient harm.

(C) is Extreme. If patients themselves aren't vaccinated, that suggests they are more susceptible to the harmful virus and thus provides a good reason why the employees should be vaccinated. However, the argument doesn't need *most* patients to be not vaccinated. Even if just a few patients are not vaccinated, they are at risk and the argument still stands.

(E) is Out of Scope. The author doesn't need society's acceptance to make this argument work, and other contexts are irrelevant.

18. (C) Inference

Step 1: Identify the Question Type
The question asks for something that the given statements "most strongly support." That makes this an Inference question.

Step 2: Untangle the Stimulus
According to the author, etiquette helps people get along with each other. There are some critics of etiquette who believe it provides no benefit. However, those critics also believe that kindness and social harmony are good.

Step 3: Make a Prediction
How could these critics say that etiquette provides no social benefit? According to the author, etiquette provides the very social harmony that such critics say is good. This suggests that the critics do not recognize the benefit of etiquette and are thus unaware that their complaint is invalid. The correct answer will be consistent with this implication.

Step 4: Evaluate the Answer Choices
(C) is correct. Because etiquette does provide a social benefit (people getting along), the critics who say otherwise are mistaken.

(A) is a Distortion. The critics actually have just one consistent view about etiquette: It provides no social benefit. The contradiction comes because of their belief about a *different* subject: social harmony. The author mentions that etiquette and social harmony are connected, but the critics don't see that. They see etiquette and social harmony as two separate ideas.

(B) is Out of Scope. There is no indication of the critics having respect for etiquette. They only show respect for kindness and social harmony, which they view as a separate issue from etiquette.

(D) is Extreme. There is no mention of etiquette being necessary, and the author makes no suggestion of how to get rid of any such need.

(E) is an Extreme Distortion. It is said that the critics *believe* that kindness and social harmony are good, but that doesn't mean they actually are. Besides, just saying they're *good* doesn't exactly support the idea that they're *highly* beneficial.

19. (D) Strengthen/Weaken (Evaluate the Argument)

Step 1: Identify the Question Type
The question asks for something "most useful ... to evaluate" the argument. That makes this an Evaluate the Argument question, which uses the skills of a Strengthen or Weaken question. The correct answer will be something relevant that could affect the validity of the argument.

Step 2: Untangle the Stimulus
The author concludes ([*t*]*hus*) that European wood ants use conifer resin to protect against diseases. The evidence is that these ants use a lot of that resin when building their nests, and that resin has been shown to kill bacteria.

Step 3: Make a Prediction
The author is committing the common error of confusing a correlation for causation. Yes, the ants use the resin. And yes, the resin has bacteria-fighting properties. However, are those properties the reason why the ants use the resin? Or, could there be an alternative explanation? The author assumes it must be for disease-fighting purposes. The correct answer will question whether it is or whether there may be an overlooked explanation.

Step 4: Evaluate the Answer Choices
(D) is correct. If the resin also provides valuable structural benefits, then that could be the reason why the ants use it. However, if it doesn't provide such benefit, then perhaps the author is right about it being used for disease protection.

(A) is Out of Scope. Without knowing how long the nests are used, knowing how long the disinfectant properties last is irrelevant. Whether the properties last a couple of months or several years, it still can't be determined whether that's the reason why ants use the resin.

(B) is an Irrelevant Comparison. It doesn't matter when the resin is used more. The argument is about why the resin is used, and this offers no way to determine whether it's for disease protection or not.

(C) is Out of Scope. Other ant species are irrelevant to the argument. The argument is about *why* these ants use the resin, not *which* ants use it.

(E) is Out of Scope. It doesn't matter why the resin evolved such disease-protecting properties. The argument is about why the ants use it, regardless of its evolutionary origin.

20. (C) Inference

Step 1: Identify the Question Type
The correct answer "must ... be true" based on the information given, making this an Inference question.

Step 2: Untangle the Stimulus
The author is discussing the difficulty in creating secure passwords. People like easy-to-remember passwords (e.g., birth dates), but those are the easiest for hackers to guess. Random passwords (e.g., r2oJ%22k) are the hardest to hack, but they're also the easiest to forget. When users forget their passwords, that takes up an administrator's time. And if a password is hard to remember, people write it down, which poses the greatest threat of all.

Step 3: Make a Prediction
"Must Be True" Inference questions often rely on Formal Logic and/or very concrete statements. There is no Formal Logic here, but there are a lot of concrete statements. Easy-to-remember passwords are the *easiest* to guess, while random passwords are the *hardest* to guess. That's useful information, and it might suggest that easy passwords are more likely to be hacked. However, the last sentence provides one more concrete statement: Passwords that are written down pose the *greatest* security threat. Because people tend to write down passwords that are difficult to remember, it's actually the random passwords, and not the easy ones, that pose the absolute greatest threat. The correct answer could use any or all of this information. Don't predict just one idea. Instead, test the choices and eliminate ones that are outside the scope or that misapply the logic.

Step 4: Evaluate the Answer Choices
(C) is correct. While easy-to-guess passwords would seem to be a major threat, the last sentence claims that the biggest threat is actually the passwords people write down—and those are the hard-to-remember ones. And if those are the greatest threat, then easy passwords must be less of a threat.

(A) is a Distortion. If writing down passwords poses the greatest security threat, then it might be wise to avoid writing them down. However, this is just a recommendation and one that is never directly addressed in the stimulus. Such a recommendation is just an opinion and can't be claimed as "must be true," no matter how reasonable it may seem based on the stimulus.

(B) is Out of Scope. While resetting passwords is said to take up administrators' time, there is no mention that this is *expensive*. Perhaps administrators would be paid the same no matter what they do, but resetting passwords just keeps them from getting other work done.

(D) is a 180. Random passwords are hard to remember and thus likely to be written down, and that poses the *greatest* threat to security.

(E) is a Distortion. The author does imply it's the hardest passwords that actually pose the greatest threat (as they get written down). However, that doesn't mean passwords get progressively more secure as they get easier. It's more likely that passwords get less secure as they get easier and more secure as they get harder to remember—until they get *too* hard and have to be written down.

21. (E) Main Point

Step 1: Identify the Question Type
The question asks for the "overall conclusion," making this a Main Point question.

Step 2: Untangle the Stimulus
The author starts off with a recommendation: If you use a wood stove in your home, it should be a wood-pellet stove instead of a regular wood stove. The rest is all evidence to support that recommendation. Wood pellets are made from by-products, which means fewer trees need to be cut down. That makes it a more environmentally friendly option.

Step 3: Make a Prediction
The Conclusion Keyword [*s*]*o* in the last sentence is a major distraction. That's the conclusion of the evidence comparing wood-pellet stoves to regular wood stoves. However, that is just a subsidiary conclusion that is ultimately used to support the recommendation in the first sentence: Homeowners should use wood-pellet stoves instead of regular wood stoves. That's the overall conclusion, as the correct answer should indicate.

Step 4: Evaluate the Answer Choices
(E) accurately identifies the opening recommendation as the conclusion.

(A) is a Faulty Use of Detail. This is just a fact that is provided as evidence for the conclusion.

(B) is a Faulty Use of Detail. This is the subsidiary conclusion at the end of the stimulus. However, this claim of environmental benefit is ultimately just a major piece of evidence in support of the overall conclusion: Wood-pellet stoves should be used instead of regular wood stoves.

(C) is a Faulty Use of Detail. This is a fact given in the stimulus that helps support the conclusion. It is not, itself, the conclusion.

(D) is a Faulty Use of Detail. When the author says "[t]he same cannot be said for regular wood stoves," that does imply that regular wood stoves require felling trees. However, that's still just a piece of evidence to support the conclusion. It's not the conclusion itself.

22. (D) Weaken

Step 1: Identify the Question Type
The question asks for something that "weakens the ... argument," making this a Weaken question.

Step 2: Untangle the Stimulus
The economist concludes that people value cash and gift cards over other gifts. The evidence is a study in which people, when asked how much they would pay for certain gifts, typically cited an amount that was only two-thirds the actual price.

Step 3: Make a Prediction
The argument commits a significant scope shift. The study shows what people would be willing to pay if they were to buy items on their own, which is lower than the actual value. However, that doesn't mean that's how they would value those items if they were received as gifts. Perhaps getting an item as a gift makes it feel *more* valuable. The economist overlooks this possibility, and the correct answer will show how people may value gifts more than the economist assumes.

Step 4: Evaluate the Answer Choices
(D) is correct. While people may not pay as much to buy the item themselves, if they got it as a gift, this suggests they wouldn't sell for it anything less than one and a half times more than it's worth. In other words, they are putting a greater value on it because it was a gift, contrary to the economist's claim.

(A) is a 180. If people are returning gifts more frequently, that could actually strengthen the economist's claims that people don't put a lot of value on those gifts.

(B) is an Irrelevant Comparison. The argument is not about which type of gift is more common. The argument is about what type of gift is perceived as more valuable by the recipient.

(C) is an Irrelevant Comparison. Even if gifts from friends and family fared better in the study than gifts from other people, the friends and family gifts still could have been valued as less than their actual price. The other gifts would just have been valued even less.

(E) is Out of Scope. What's required to return items is irrelevant to how people value those items.

23. (E) Paradox

Step 1: Identify the Question Type
The question asks for something that would "help to explain" a situation, making this a Paradox question.

Step 2: Untangle the Stimulus
The author mentions a new antitheft device: a homing beacon that helps track stolen cars. It doesn't directly deter thieves, as they can't tell which cars have the device, but it does improve the chances of catching the thieves if they do steal the car. However, even though very few cars have the beacon, auto thefts have dropped dramatically in cities where it's used.

Step 3: Make a Prediction
The mystery is revealed at the end: If so few cars are equipped with this beacon, then how are auto thefts decreasing so dramatically? It's given that the devices are effective in catching thieves. Perhaps this effectiveness is somehow deterring thieves from even trying. The correct answer will provide information that shows how this could be happening, despite how few beacons are installed.

Step 4: Evaluate the Answer Choices
(E) is correct. If most thefts are committed by a select few thieves, then only those few people need to be caught. If those few thieves can be captured thanks to the effective beacon in just a few random cars, then that would be enough to drop the rate considerably.

(A) is a Distortion. This might show why the device is so effective when it's used. The thieves are careless and thus easier to capture. However, it still doesn't explain why the theft rate would drop so dramatically if so few cars actually have the beacon.

(B) is a Distortion. This just suggests that the cities in which the beacon is used were already low-theft areas to begin with. However, that doesn't explain why that already low rate dropped so dramatically after installing just a few beacons.

(C) is a Distortion. If the beacons are making apprehensions more likely, that could help explain some decrease in thefts. However, it still doesn't explain why the decrease was so dramatic after installing the beacons in such a small percentage of cars.

(D) is Out of Scope. It doesn't matter where the thieves live. The mystery is only about where the cars are located and what caused the theft rate to drop so dramatically.

24. (D) Flaw

Step 1: Identify the Question Type
The question asks why the argument is "vulnerable to criticism," which is common wording for a Flaw question.

Step 2: Untangle the Stimulus
The author concludes ([*s*]*o*) that the Internet will eventually have humanlike intelligence. The evidence is that the computers that form the Internet transmit information in the same way as the neurons that form our brain, and the Internet is just getting bigger and bigger.

Step 3: Make a Prediction
This argument hinges on a major scope shift. The Internet mimics our brain in the way it transmits information. However, does that really mean it's getting humanlike

intelligence? That's a big leap, and the correct answer will expose this gap between transmitting information and exhibiting intelligence.

Step 4: Evaluate the Answer Choices

(D) is correct. This describes how the author provides no evidence that the ability to transmit information is enough to warrant a conclusion about computers gaining humanlike intelligence.

(A) is a Distortion. It's not the complexity of the Internet that is equated to intelligence. It's the way in which the Internet transmits information that mimic our brain's neurons.

(B) is Out of Scope. The author isn't arguing that the Internet will be the *first* technology to mimic human intelligence. The author is just saying the Internet will, whether or not it's the first technology to do so.

(C) is a Distortion. There's no reason to suggest that the analogy between the computers and our neurons is faulty. That might be a valid analogy. The flaw is that this analogy is then used to support a claim about human intelligence, which is not warranted.

(E) is Out of Scope. It doesn't matter if people are interested in making this happen or not. The argument is only about whether or not it will happen.

25. (C) Strengthen

Step 1: Identify the Question Type

The question asks for something that will "most strengthen" the argument, making this a Strengthen question.

Step 2: Untangle the Stimulus

According to the editorial, division of income classes is a problem for democratic societies. People get stuck in their class, unable to move from one class to another. This leads to political factions and poor governing. But the editorial proposes a solution: encourage economic expansion, since that would allow people to improve their economic standing.

Step 3: Make a Prediction

Helping people improve their economic standing would certainly help them break out of their income class and into a new one. Unfortunately, this only solves half the problem. If *everyone* improves and breaks into a new class, everybody will still be divided the same—just with higher incomes. And it's the division that really causes problems. To make this proposal stronger, it should be shown how economic expansion won't just create the same divisions as before.

Step 4: Evaluate the Answer Choices

(C) is correct. This suggests that not everybody will increase the same. The people with the lowest income are more likely to bump up and move into a new class, while people at higher levels are less likely to move and more likely to stay put. That means different, and possibly fewer and better, divisions.

(A) is a 180, at worst. This suggests another factor that needs to be addressed: discord. If economic expansion doesn't address discord, then it may not work as well as the editorial claims.

(B) is a Distortion. This suggests that it may be feasible to adopt economic expansion policies, but that doesn't mean they'll work.

(D) is Out of Scope. This just provides a requirement for economic expansion, which won't help the argument at all. The argument is about whether or not that expansion will help, regardless of what is required to do it.

(E) is Out of Scope. Any obstacles to economic expansion have no bearing on whether or not such policies will help should they overcome those obstacles.

Glossary

Logical Reasoning

Logical Reasoning Question Types

Argument-Based Questions

Main Point Question

A question that asks for an argument's conclusion or an author's main point. Typical question stems:

> Which one of the following most accurately expresses the conclusion of the argument as a whole?

> Which one of the following sentences best expresses the main point of the scientist's argument?

Role of a Statement Question

A question that asks how a specific sentence, statement, or idea functions within an argument. Typical question stems:

> Which one of the following most accurately describes the role played in the argument by the statement that automation within the steel industry allowed steel mills to produce more steel with fewer workers?

> The claim that governmental transparency is a nation's primary defense against public-sector corruption figures in the argument in which one of the following ways?

Point at Issue Question

A question that asks you to identify the specific claim, statement, or recommendation about which two speakers/authors disagree (or, rarely, about which they agree). Typical question stems:

> A point at issue between Tom and Jerry is

> The dialogue most strongly supports the claim that Marilyn and Billy disagree with each other about which one of the following?

Method of Argument Question

A question that asks you to describe an author's argumentative strategy. In other words, the correct answer describes *how* the author argues (not necessarily what the author says). Typical question stems:

> Which one of the following most accurately describes the technique of reasoning employed by the argument?

> Julian's argument proceeds by

> In the dialogue, Alexander responds to Abigail in which one of the following ways?

Parallel Reasoning Question

A question that asks you to identify the answer choice containing an argument that has the same logical structure and reaches the same type of conclusion as the argument in the stimulus does. Typical question stems:

> The pattern of reasoning in which one of the following arguments is most parallel to that in the argument above?

> The pattern of reasoning in which one of the following arguments is most similar to the pattern of reasoning in the argument above?

Assumption-Family Questions

Assumption Question

A question that asks you to identify one of the unstated premises in an author's argument. Assumption questions come in two varieties.

Necessary Assumption questions ask you to identify an unstated premise required for an argument's conclusion to follow logically from its evidence. Typical question stems:

> Which one of the following is an assumption on which the argument depends?

> Which one of the following is an assumption that the argument requires in order for its conclusion to be properly drawn?

Sufficient Assumption questions ask you to identify an unstated premise sufficient to establish the argument's conclusion on the basis of its evidence. Typical question stems:

> The conclusion follows logically if which one of the following is assumed?

> Which one of the following, if assumed, enables the conclusion above to be properly inferred?

Strengthen/Weaken Question

A question that asks you to identify a fact that, if true, would make the argument's conclusion more likely (Strengthen) or less likely (Weaken) to follow from its evidence. Typical question stems:

Strengthen

Which one of the following, if true, most strengthens the argument above?

Which one the following, if true, most strongly supports the claim above?

Weaken

Which one of the following, if true, would most weaken the argument above?

Which one of the following, if true, most calls into question the claim above?

Flaw Question

A question that asks you to describe the reasoning error that the author has made in an argument. Typical question stems:

The argument's reasoning is most vulnerable to criticism on the grounds that the argument

Which of the following identifies a reasoning error in the argument?

The reasoning in the correspondent's argument is questionable because the argument

Parallel Flaw Question

A question that asks you to identify the argument that contains the same error(s) in reasoning that the argument in the stimulus contains. Typical question stems:

The pattern of flawed reasoning exhibited by the argument above is most similar to that exhibited in which one of the following?

Which one of the following most closely parallels the questionable reasoning cited above?

Evaluate the Argument Question

A question that asks you to identify an issue or consideration relevant to the validity of an argument. Think of Evaluate questions as "Strengthen or Weaken" questions. The correct answer, if true, will strengthen the argument, and if false, will weaken the argument, or vice versa. Evaluate questions are very rare. Typical question stems:

Which one of the following would be most useful to know in order to evaluate the legitimacy of the professor's argument?

It would be most important to determine which one of the following in evaluating the argument?

Non-Argument Questions

Inference Question

A question that asks you to identify a statement that follows from the statements in the stimulus. It is very important to note the characteristics of the one correct and the four incorrect answers before evaluating the choices in Inference questions. Depending on the wording of the question stem, the correct answer to an Inference question may be the one that

- *must be true* if the statements in the stimulus are true

- is *most strongly supported* by the statements in the stimulus

- *must be false* if the statements in the stimulus are true

Typical question stems:

If all of the statements above are true, then which one of the following must also be true?

Which one of the following can be properly inferred from the information above?

If the statements above are true, then each of the following could be true EXCEPT:

Which one of the following is most strongly supported by the information above?

The statements above, if true, most support which one of the following?

The facts described above provide the strongest evidence against which one of the following?

Paradox Question

A question that asks you to identify a fact that, if true, most helps to explain, resolve, or reconcile an apparent contradiction. Typical question stems:

Which one of the following, if true, most helps to explain how both studies' findings could be accurate?

Which one the following, if true, most helps to resolve the apparent conflict in the spokesperson's statements?

Each one of the following, if true, would contribute to an explanation of the apparent discrepancy in the information above EXCEPT:

Principle Questions

Principle Question

A question that asks you to identify corresponding cases and principles. Some Principle questions provide a principle in the stimulus and call for the answer choice describing a case that corresponds to the principle. Others provide a specific case in the stimulus and call for the answer containing a principle to which that case corresponds.

On the LSAT, Principle questions almost always mirror the skills rewarded by other Logical Reasoning question types. After each of the following Principle question stems, we note the question type it resembles. Typical question stems:

> Which one of the following principles, if valid, most helps to justify the reasoning above? (**Strengthen**)

> Which one of the following most accurately expresses the principle underlying the reasoning above? (**Assumption**)

> The situation described above most closely conforms to which of the following generalizations? (**Inference**)

> Which one of the following situations conforms most closely to the principle described above? (**Inference**)

> Which one of the following principles, if valid, most helps to reconcile the apparent conflict among the prosecutor's claims? (**Paradox**)

Parallel Principle Question

A question that asks you to identify a specific case that illustrates the same principle that is illustrated by the case described in the stimulus. Typical question stem:

> Of the following, which one illustrates a principle that is most similar to the principle illustrated by the passage?

Untangling the Stimulus

Conclusion Types

The conclusions in arguments found in the Logical Reasoning section of the LSAT tend to fall into one of six categories:

1) Value Judgment (an evaluative statement; e.g., Action X is unethical, or Y's recital was poorly sung)

2) "If"/Then (a conditional prediction, recommendation, or assertion; e.g., If X is true, then so is Y, or If you are M, then you should do N)

3) Prediction (X *will* or *will not* happen in the future)

4) Comparison (X is taller/shorter/more common/less common, etc. than Y)

5) Assertion of Fact (X is true or X is false)

6) Recommendation (we *should* or *should not* do X)

One-Sentence Test

A tactic used to identify the author's conclusion in an argument. Consider which sentence in the argument is the one the author would keep if asked to get rid of everything except her main point.

Subsidiary Conclusion

A conclusion following from one piece of evidence and then used by the author to support his overall conclusion or main point. Consider the following argument:

> The pharmaceutical company's new experimental treatment did not succeed in clinical trials. As a result, the new treatment will not reach the market this year. Thus, the company will fall short of its revenue forecasts for the year.

Here, the sentence "As a result, the new treatment will not reach the market this year" is a subsidiary conclusion. It follows from the evidence that the new treatment failed in clinical trials, and it provides evidence for the overall conclusion that the company will not meet its revenue projections.

Keyword(s) in Logical Reasoning

A word or phrase that helps you untangle a question's stimulus by indicating the logical structure of the argument or the author's point. Here are three categories of Keywords to which LSAT experts pay special attention in Logical Reasoning:

Conclusion words; e.g., *therefore, thus, so, as a result, it follows that, consequently*, [evidence] *is evidence that* [conclusion]

Evidence words; e.g., *because, since, after all, for*, [evidence] *is evidence that* [conclusion]

Contrast words; e.g., *but, however, while, despite, in spite of, on the other hand* (These are especially useful in Paradox and Inference questions.)

Experts use Keywords even more extensively in Reading Comprehension. Learn the Keywords associated with the Reading Comprehension section, and apply them to Logical Reasoning when they are helpful.

Mismatched Concepts

One of two patterns to which authors' assumptions conform in LSAT arguments. Mismatched Concepts describes the assumption in arguments in which terms or concepts in the conclusion are different *in kind* from those in the evidence. The author assumes that there is a logical relationship between the different terms. For example:

> Bobby is a **championship swimmer**. Therefore, he **trains every day**.

Here, the words "trains every day" appear only in the conclusion, and the words "championship swimmer" appear only in the evidence. For the author to reach this conclusion from this evidence, he assumes that championship swimmers train every day.

Another example:

Susan does **not eat her vegetables**. Thus, she will **not grow big and strong**.

In this argument, not growing big and strong is found only in the conclusion while not eating vegetables is found only in the evidence. For the author to reach this conclusion from this evidence, she must assume that eating one's vegetables is necessary for one to grow big and strong.

See also Overlooked Possibilities.

Overlooked Possibilities

One of two patterns to which authors' assumptions conform in LSAT arguments. Overlooked Possibilities describes the assumption in arguments in which terms or concepts in the conclusion are different *in degree, scale, or level of certainty* from those in the evidence. The author assumes that there is no factor or explanation for the conclusion other than the one(s) offered in the evidence. For example:

Samson does not have a ticket stub for this movie showing. Thus, Samson must have sneaked into the movie without paying.

The author assumes that there is no other explanation for Samson's lack of a ticket stub. The author overlooks several possibilities: e.g., Samson had a special pass for this showing of the movie; Samson dropped his ticket stub by accident or threw it away after entering the theater; someone else in Samson's party has all of the party members' ticket stubs in her pocket or handbag.

Another example:

Jonah's marketing plan will save the company money. Therefore, the company should adopt Jonah's plan.

Here, the author makes a recommendation based on one advantage. The author assumes that the advantage is the company's only concern or that there are no disadvantages that could outweigh it, e.g., Jonah's plan might save money on marketing but not generate any new leads or customers; Jonah's plan might damage the company's image or reputation; Jonah's plan might include illegal false advertising. Whenever the author of an LSAT argument concludes with a recommendation or a prediction based on just a single fact in the evidence, that author is always overlooking many other possibilities.

See also Mismatched Concepts.

Causal Argument

An argument in which the author concludes or assumes that one thing causes another. The most common pattern on the LSAT is for the author to conclude that A causes B from evidence that A and B are correlated. For example:

I notice that whenever the store has a poor sales month, employee tardiness is also higher that month. Therefore, it must be that employee tardiness causes the store to lose sales.

The author assumes that the correlation in the evidence indicates a causal relationship. These arguments are vulnerable to three types of overlooked possibilities:

1) There could be **another causal factor**. In the previous example, maybe the months in question are those in which the manager takes vacation, causing the store to lose sales and permitting employees to arrive late without fear of the boss's reprimands.

2) Causation could be **reversed**. Maybe in months when sales are down, employee morale suffers and tardiness increases as a result.

3) The correlation could be **coincidental**. Maybe the correlation between tardiness and the dip in sales is pure coincidence.

See also Flaw Types: Correlation versus Causation.

Another pattern in causal arguments (less frequent on the LSAT) involves the assumption that a particular causal mechanism is or is not involved in a causal relationship. For example:

The airport has rerouted takeoffs and landings so that they will not create noise over the Sunnyside neighborhood. Thus, the recent drop in Sunnyside's property values cannot be explained by the neighborhood's proximity to the airport.

Here, the author assumes that the only way that the airport could be the cause of dropping property values is through noise pollution. The author overlooks any other possible mechanism (e.g., frequent traffic jams and congestion) through which proximity to the airport could be the cause of Sunnyside's woes.

Principle

A broad, law-like rule, definition, or generalization that covers a variety of specific cases with defined attributes. To see how principles are treated on the LSAT, consider the following principle:

It is immoral for a person for his own gain to mislead another person.

That principle would cover a specific case, such as a seller who lies about the quality of construction to get a higher price for his house. It would also correspond to the case of a teenager who, wishing to spend a night out on the town, tells his mom "I'm going over to Randy's house." He knows that his mom believes that he will be staying at Randy's house, when in fact, he and Randy will go out together.

That principle does not, however, cover cases in which someone lies solely for the purpose of making the other person feel better or in which one person inadvertently misleads the other through a mistake of fact.

Be careful not to apply your personal ethics or morals when analyzing the principles articulated on the test.

Flaw Types

Necessary versus Sufficient

This flaw occurs when a speaker or author concludes that one event is necessary for a second event from evidence that the first event is sufficient to bring about the second event, or vice versa. Example:

> If more than 25,000 users attempt to access the new app at the same time, the server will crash. Last night, at 11:15 PM, the server crashed, so it must be the case that more than 25,000 users were attempting to use the new app at that time.

In making this argument, the author assumes that the only thing that will cause the server to crash is the usage level (i.e., high usage is *necessary* for the server to crash). The evidence, however, says that high usage is one thing that will cause the server to crash (i.e., that high usage is *sufficient* to crash the server).

Correlation versus Causation

This flaw occurs when a speaker or author draws a conclusion that one thing causes another from evidence that the two things are correlated. Example:

> Over the past half century, global sugar consumption has tripled. That same time period has seen a surge in the rate of technological advancement worldwide. It follows that the increase in sugar consumption has caused the acceleration in technological advancement.

In any argument with this structure, the author is making three unwarranted assumptions. First, he assumes that there is no alternate cause, i.e., there is nothing else that has contributed to rapid technological advancement. Second, he assumes that the causation is not reversed, i.e., technological advancement has not contributed to the increase in sugar consumption, perhaps by making it easier to grow, refine, or transport sugar. And, third, he assumes that the two phenomena are not merely coincidental, i.e., that it is not just happenstance that global sugar consumption is up at the same time that the pace of technological advancement has accelerated.

Unrepresentative Sample

This flaw occurs when a speaker or author draws a conclusion about a group from evidence in which the sample cannot represent that group because the sample is too small or too selective, or is biased in some way. Example:

> Moviegoers in our town prefer action films and romantic comedies over other film genres. Last Friday, we sent reporters to survey moviegoers at several theaters in town, and nearly 90 percent of those surveyed were going to watch either an action film or a romantic comedy.

The author assumes that the survey was representative of the town's moviegoers, but there are several reasons to question that assumption. First, we don't know how many people were actually surveyed. Even if the number of people surveyed was adequate, we don't know how many other types of movies were playing. Finally, the author doesn't limit her conclusion to moviegoers on Friday nights. If the survey had been conducted at Sunday matinees, maybe most moviegoers would have been heading out to see an animated family film or a historical drama. Who knows?

Scope Shift/Unwarranted Assumption

This flaw occurs when a speaker's or author's evidence has a scope or has terms different enough from the scope or terms in his conclusion that it is doubtful that the evidence can support the conclusion. Example:

> A very small percentage of working adults in this country can correctly define collateralized debt obligation securities. Thus, sad to say, the majority of the nation's working adults cannot make prudent choices about how to invest their savings.

This speaker assumes that prudent investing requires the ability to accurately define a somewhat obscure financial term. But prudence is not the same thing as expertise, and the speaker does not offer any evidence that this knowledge of this particular term is related to wise investing.

Percent versus Number/Rate versus Number

This flaw occurs when a speaker or author draws a conclusion about real quantities from evidence about rates or percentages, or vice versa. Example:

> At the end of last season, Camp SunnyDay laid off half of their senior counselors and a quarter of their junior counselors. Thus, Camp SunnyDay must have more senior counselors than junior counselors.

The problem, of course, is that we don't know how many senior and junior counselors were on staff before the layoffs. If there were a total of 4 senior counselors and 20 junior counselors, then the camp would have laid off only 2 senior counselors while dismissing 5 junior counselors.

Equivocation

This flaw occurs when a speaker or author uses the same word in two different and incompatible ways. Example:

> Our opponent in the race has accused our candidate's staff members of behaving unprofessionally. But that's not fair. Our staff is made up entirely of volunteers, not paid campaign workers.

The speaker interprets the opponent's use of the word *professional* to mean "paid," but the opponent likely meant something more along the lines of "mature, competent, and businesslike."

Ad Hominem

This flaw occurs when a speaker or author concludes that another person's claim or argument is invalid because that other person has a personal flaw or shortcoming. One common pattern is for the speaker or author to claim the other person acts hypocritically or that the other person's claim is made from self-interest. Example:

> Mrs. Smithers testified before the city council, stating that the speed limits on the residential streets near her home are dangerously high. But why should we give her claim any credence? The way she eats and exercises, she's not even looking out for her own health.

The author attempts to undermine Mrs. Smithers's testimony by attacking her character and habits. He doesn't offer any evidence that is relevant to her claim about speed limits.

Part versus Whole

This flaw occurs when a speaker or author concludes that a part or individual has a certain characteristic because the whole or the larger group has that characteristic, or vice versa. Example:

> Patient: I should have no problems taking the three drugs prescribed to me by my doctors. I looked them up, and none of the three is listed as having any major side effects.

Here, the patient is assuming that what is true of each of the drugs individually will be true of them when taken together. The patient's flaw is overlooking possible interactions that could cause problems not present when the drugs are taken separately.

Circular Reasoning

This flaw occurs when a speaker or author tries to prove a conclusion with evidence that is logically equivalent to the conclusion. Example:

> All those who run for office are prevaricators. To see this, just consider politicians: they all prevaricate.

Perhaps the author has tried to disguise the circular reasoning in this argument by exchanging the words "those who run for office" in the conclusion for "politicians" in the evidence, but all this argument amounts to is "Politicians prevaricate; therefore, politicians prevaricate." On the LSAT, circular reasoning is very rarely the correct answer to a Flaw question, although it is regularly described in one of the wrong answers.

Question Strategies

Denial Test

A tactic for identifying the assumption *necessary* to an argument. When you negate an assumption necessary to an argument, the argument will fall apart. Negating an assumption that is not necessary to the argument will not invalidate the argument. Consider the following argument:

> Only high schools that produced a state champion athlete during the school year will be represented at the Governor's awards banquet. Therefore, McMurtry High School will be represented at the Governor's awards banquet.

Which one of the following is an assumption necessary to that argument?

> (1) McMurtry High School produced more state champion athletes than any other high school during the school year.
>
> (2) McMurtry High School produced at least one state champion athlete during the school year.

If you are at all confused about which of those two statements reflects the *necessary* assumption, negate them both.

> (1) McMurtry High School **did not produce more** state champion athletes than any other high school during the school year.

That does not invalidate the argument. McMurtry could still be represented at the Governor's banquet.

> (2) McMurtry High School **did not produce any** state champion athletes during the school year.

Here, negating the statement causes the argument to fall apart. Statement (2) is an assumption *necessary* to the argument.

Point at Issue "Decision Tree"

A tactic for evaluating the answer choices in Point at Issue questions. The correct answer is the only answer choice to which you can answer "Yes" to all three questions in the following diagram.

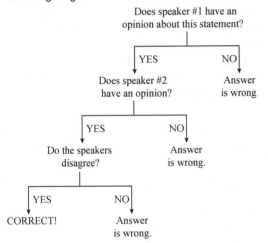

Common Methods of Argument

These methods of argument or argumentative strategies are common on the LSAT:

- Analogy, in which an author draws parallels between two unrelated (but purportedly similar) situations
- Example, in which an author cites a specific case or cases to justify a generalization
- Counterexample, in which an author seeks to discredit an opponent's argument by citing a specific case or cases that appear to invalidate the opponent's generalization
- Appeal to authority, in which an author cites an expert's claim or opinion as support for her conclusion
- Ad hominem attack, in which an author attacks her opponent's personal credibility rather than attacking the substance of her opponent's argument
- Elimination of alternatives, in which an author lists possibilities and discredits or rules out all but one
- Means/requirements, in which the author argues that something is needed to achieve a desired result

Wrong Answer Types in LR

Outside the Scope (Out of Scope; Beyond the Scope)

An answer choice containing a statement that is too broad, too narrow, or beyond the purview of the stimulus, making the statement in the choice irrelevant

180

An answer choice that directly contradicts what the correct answer must say (e.g., a choice that strengthens the argument in a Weaken question)

Extreme

An answer choice containing language too emphatic to be supported by the stimulus; often (although not always) characterized by words such as *all*, *never*, *every*, *only*, or *most*

Distortion

An answer choice that mentions details from the stimulus but mangles or misstates what the author said about those details

Irrelevant Comparison

An answer choice that compares two items or attributes in a way not germane to the author's argument or statements

Half-Right/Half-Wrong

An answer choice that begins correctly, but then contradicts or distorts the passage in its second part; this wrong answer type is more common in Reading Comprehension than it is in Logical Reasoning

Faulty Use of Detail

An answer choice that accurately states something from the stimulus, but does so in a manner that answers the question incorrectly; this wrong answer type is more common in Reading Comprehension than it is in Logical Reasoning

Logic Games

Game Types

Strict Sequencing Game

A game that asks you to arrange entities into numbered positions or into a set schedule (usually hours or days). Strict Sequencing is, by far, the most common game type on the LSAT. In the typical Strict Sequencing game, there is a one-to-one matchup of entities and positions, e.g., seven entities to be placed in seven positions, one per position, or six entities to be placed over six consecutive days, one entity per day.

From time to time, the LSAT will offer Strict Sequencing with more entities than positions (e.g., seven entities to be arranged over five days, with some days to receive more than one entity) or more positions than entities (e.g., six entities to be scheduled over seven days, with at least one day to receive no entities).

Other, less common variations on Strict Sequencing include:

Double Sequencing, in which each entity is placed or scheduled two times (there have been rare occurrences of Triple or Quadruple Sequencing). Alternatively, a Double Sequencing game may involve two different sets of entities each sequenced once.

Circular Sequencing, in which entities are arranged around a table or in a circular arrangement (NOTE: When the positions in a Circular Sequencing game are numbered, the first and last positions are adjacent.)

Vertical Sequencing, in which the positions are numbered from top to bottom or from bottom to top (as in the floors of a building)

Loose Sequencing Game

A game that asks you to arrange or schedule entities in order but provides no numbering or naming of the positions. The rules in Loose Sequencing give only the relative positions (earlier or later, higher or lower) between two entities or among three entities. Loose Sequencing games almost always provide that there will be no ties between entities in the rank, order, or position they take.

Circular Sequencing Game

See Strict Sequencing Game.

Selection Game

A game that asks you to choose or include some entities from the initial list of entities and to reject or exclude others. Some Selection games provide overall limitations on the number of entities to be selected (e.g., "choose exactly four of seven students" or "choose at least two of six entrees") while others provide little or no restriction on the number selected ("choose at least one type of flower" or "select from among seven board members").

Distribution Game

A game that asks you to break up the initial list of entities into two, three, or (very rarely) four groups or teams. In the vast majority of Distribution games, each entity is assigned to one and only one group or team. A relatively common variation on Distribution games will provide a subdivided list of entities (e.g., eight students—four men and four women—will form

three study groups) and will then require representatives from those subdivisions on each team (e.g., each study group will have at least one of the men on it).

Matching Game

A game that asks you to match one or more members of one set of entities to specific members of another set of entities, or that asks you to match attributes or objects to a set of entities. Unlike Distribution games, in which each entity is placed in exactly one group or team, Matching games usually permit you to assign the same attribute or object to more than one entity.

In some cases, there are overall limitations on the number of entities that can be matched (e.g., "In a school's wood shop, there are four workstations—numbered 1 through 4—and each workstation has at least one and at most three of the following tools—band saw, dremmel tool, electric sander, and power drill"). In almost all Matching games, further restrictions on the number of entities that can be matched to a particular person or place will be found in the rules (e.g., Workstation 4 will have more tools than Workstation 2 has).

Hybrid Game

A game that asks you to do two (or rarely, three) of the standard actions (Sequencing, Selection, Distribution, and Matching) to a set of entities.

The most common Hybrid is Sequencing-Matching. A typical Sequencing-Matching Hybrid game might ask you to schedule six speakers at a conference to six one-hour speaking slots (from 9 AM to 2 PM), and then assign each speaker one of two subjects (economic development or trade policy).

Nearly as common as Sequencing-Matching is Distribution-Sequencing. A typical game of this type might ask you to divide six people in a talent competition into either a Dance category or a Singing category, and then rank the competitors in each category.

It is most common to see one Hybrid game in each Logic Games section, although there have been tests with two Hybrid games and tests with none. To determine the type of Hybrid you are faced with, identify the game's action in Step 1 of the Logic Games Method. For example, a game asking you to choose four of six runners, and then assign the four chosen runners to lanes numbered 1 through 4 on a track, would be a Selection-Sequencing Hybrid game.

Mapping Game

A game that provides you with a description of geographical locations and, typically, of the connections among them. Mapping games often ask you to determine the shortest possible routes between two locations or to account for the number of connections required to travel from one location to another. This game type is extremely rare, and as of February 2017, a Mapping game was last seen on PrepTest 40 administered in June 2003.

Process Game

A game that opens with an initial arrangement of entities (e.g., a starting sequence or grouping) and provides rules that describe the processes through which that arrangement can be altered. The questions typically ask you for acceptable arrangements or placements of particular entities after one, two, or three stages in the process. Occasionally, a Process game question might provide information about the arrangement after one, two, or three stages in the process and ask you what must have happened in the earlier stages. This game type is extremely rare, and as of November 2016, a Process game was last seen on PrepTest 16 administered in September 1995. However, there was a Process game on PrepTest 80, administered in December 2016, thus ending a 20-year hiatus.

Game Setups and Deductions

Floater

An entity that is not restricted by any rule or limitation in the game

Blocks of Entities

Two or more entities that are required by rule to be adjacent or separated by a set number of spaces (Sequencing games), to be placed together in the same group (Distribution games), to be matched to the same entity (Matching games), or to be selected or rejected together (Selection games)

Limited Options

Rules or restrictions that force all of a game's acceptable arrangements into two (or occasionally three) patterns

Established Entities

An entity required by rule to be placed in one space or assigned to one particular group throughout the entire game

Number Restrictions

Rules or limitations affecting the number of entities that may be placed into a group or space throughout the game

Duplications

Two or more rules that restrict a common entity. Usually, these rules can be combined to reach additional deductions. For example, if you know that B is placed earlier than A in a sequence and that C is placed earlier than B in that sequence, you can deduce that C is placed earlier than A in the sequence and that there is at least one space (the space occupied by B) between C and A.

Master Sketch

The final sketch derived from the game's setup, rules, and deductions. LSAT experts preserve the Master Sketch for reference as they work through the questions. The Master Sketch does not include any conditions from New-"If" question stems.

Logic Games Question Types

Acceptability Question

A question in which the correct answer is an acceptable arrangement of all the entities relative to the spaces, groups, or selection criteria in the game. Answer these by using the rules to eliminate answer choices that violate the rules.

Partial Acceptability Question

A question in which the correct answer is an acceptable arrangement of some of the entities relative to some of the spaces, groups, or selection criteria in the game, and in which the arrangement of entities not included in the answer choices could be acceptable to the spaces, groups, or selection criteria not explicitly shown in the answer choices. Answer these the same way you would answer Acceptability questions, by using the rules to eliminate answer choices that explicitly or implicitly violate the rules.

Must Be True/False; Could Be True/False Question

A question in which the correct answer must be true, could be true, could be false, or must be false (depending on the question stem), and in which no additional rules or conditions are provided by the question stem

New-"If" Question

A question in which the stem provides an additional rule, condition, or restriction (applicable only to that question), and then asks what must/could be true/false as a result. LSAT experts typically handle New-"If" questions by copying the Master Sketch, adding the new restriction to the copy, and working out any additional deductions available as a result of the new restriction before evaluating the answer choices.

Rule Substitution Question

A question in which the correct answer is a rule that would have an impact identical to one of the game's original rules on the entities in the game

Rule Change Question

A question in which the stem alters one of the original rules in the game, and then asks what must/could be true/false as a result. LSAT experts typically handle Rule Change questions by reconstructing the game's sketch, but now accounting for the changed rule in place of the original. These questions are rare on recent tests.

Rule Suspension Question

A question in which the stem indicates that you should ignore one of the original rules in the game, and then asks what must/could be true/false as a result. LSAT experts typically handle Rule Suspension questions by reconstructing the game's sketch, but now accounting for the absent rule. These questions are very rare.

Complete and Accurate List Question

A question in which the correct answer is a list of any and all entities that could acceptably appear in a particular space or group, or a list of any and all spaces or groups in which a particular entity could appear

Completely Determine Question

A question in which the correct answer is a condition that would result in exactly one acceptable arrangement for all of the entities in the game

Supply the "If" Question

A question in which the correct answer is a condition that would guarantee a particular result stipulated in the question stem

Minimum/Maximum Question

A question in which the correct answer is the number corresponding to the fewest or greatest number of entities that could be selected (Selection), placed into a particular group (Distribution), or matched to a particular entity (Matching). Often, Minimum/Maximum questions begin with New-"If" conditions.

Earliest/Latest Question

A question in which the correct answer is the earliest or latest position in which an entity may acceptably be placed. Often, Earliest/Latest questions begin with New-"If" conditions.

"How Many" Question

A question in which the correct answer is the exact number of entities that may acceptably be placed into a particular group or space. Often, "How Many" questions begin with New-"If" conditions.

Reading Comprehension

Strategic Reading

Roadmap

The test taker's markup of the passage text in Step 1 (Read the Passage Strategically) of the Reading Comprehension Method. To create helpful Roadmaps, LSAT experts circle or underline Keywords in the passage text and jot down brief, helpful notes or paragraph summaries in the margin of their test booklets.

Keyword(s) in Reading Comprehension

Words in the passage text that reveal the passage structure or the author's point of view and thus help test takers anticipate and research the questions that accompany the passage. LSAT experts pay attention to six categories of Keywords in Reading Comprehension:

Emphasis/Opinion—words that signal that the author finds a detail noteworthy or that the author has positive or negative opinion about a detail; any subjective or evaluative language on the author's part (e.g., *especially*, *crucial*, *unfortunately*, *disappointing*, *I suggest*, *it seems likely*)

Contrast—words indicating that the author finds two details or ideas incompatible or that the two details illustrate conflicting points (e.g., *but*, *yet*, *despite*, *on the other hand*)

Logic—words that indicate an argument, either the author's or someone else's; these include both Evidence and Conclusion Keywords (e.g., *thus*, *therefore*, *because*, *it follows that*)

Illustration—words indicating an example offered to clarify or support another point (e.g., *for example*, *this shows*, *to illustrate*)

Sequence/Chronology—words showing steps in a process or developments over time (e.g., *traditionally*, *in the past*, *today*, *first*, *second*, *finally*, *earlier*, *subsequent*)

Continuation—words indicating that a subsequent example or detail supports the same point or illustrates the same idea as the previous example (e.g., *moreover*, *in addition*, *also*, *further*, *along the same lines*)

Margin Notes

The brief notes or paragraph summaries that the test taker jots down next to the passage in the margin of the test booklet

Big Picture Summaries: Topic/Scope/Purpose/Main Idea

A test taker's mental summary of the passage as a whole made during Step 1 (Read the Passage Strategically) of the Reading Comprehension Method. LSAT experts account for four aspects of the passage in their big picture summaries:

Topic—the overall subject of the passage

Scope—the particular aspect of the Topic that the author focuses on

Purpose—the author's reason or motive for writing the passage (express this as a verb; e.g., *to refute*, *to outline*, *to evaluate*, *to critique*)

Main Idea—the author's conclusion or overall takeaway; if the passage does not contain an explicit conclusion or thesis, you can combine the author's Scope and Purpose to get a good sense of the Main Idea.

Passage Types

Kaplan categorizes Reading Comprehension passages in two ways, by subject matter and by passage structure.

Subject matter categories

In the majority of LSAT Reading Comprehension sections, there is one passage from each of the following subject matter categories:

Humanities—topics from art, music, literature, philosophy, etc.

Natural Science—topics from biology, astronomy, paleontology, physics, etc.

Social Science—topics from anthropology, history, sociology, psychology, etc.

Law—topics from constitutional law, international law, legal education, jurisprudence, etc.

Passage structure categories

The majority of LSAT Reading Comprehension passages correspond to one of the following descriptions. The first categories—Theory/Perspective and Event/ Phenomenon—have been the most common on recent LSATs.

Theory/Perspective—The passage focuses on a thinker's theory or perspective on some aspect of the Topic; typically (though not always), the author disagrees and critiques the thinker's perspective and/or defends his own perspective.

Event/Phenomenon—The passage focuses on an event, a breakthrough development, or a problem that has recently arisen; when a solution to the problem is proposed, the author most often agrees with the solution (and that represents the passage's Main Idea).

Biography—The passage discusses something about a notable person; the aspect of the person's life emphasized by the author reflects the Scope of the passage.

Debate—The passage outlines two opposing positions (neither of which is the author's) on some aspect of the Topic; the author may side with one of the positions, may remain neutral, or may critique both. (This structure has been relatively rare on recent LSATs.)

Comparative Reading

A pair of passages (labeled Passage A and Passage B) that stand in place of the typical single passage; they have appeared exactly one time in each Reading Comprehension section administered since June 2007. The paired Comparative Reading passages share the same Topic, but may have different Scopes and Purposes. On most LSAT tests, a majority of the questions accompanying Comparative Reading passages require the test taker to compare or contrast ideas or details from both passages.

Question Strategies

Research Clues

A reference in a Reading Comprehension question stem to a word, phrase, or detail in the passage text, or to a particular line number or paragraph in the passage. LSAT experts recognize five kinds of research clues:

Line Reference—An LSAT expert researches around the referenced lines, looking for Keywords that indicate why the referenced details were included or how they were used by the author.

Paragraph Reference—An LSAT expert consults her passage Roadmap to see the paragraph's Scope and Purpose.

Quoted Text (often accompanied by a line reference)—An LSAT expert checks the context of the quoted term or phrase, asking what the author meant by it in the passage.

Proper Nouns—An LSAT expert checks the context of the person, place, or thing in the passage, asking whether the author made a positive, negative, or neutral evaluation of it and why the author included it in the passage.

Content Clues—These are terms, concepts, or ideas from the passage mentioned in the question stem but not as direct quotes and not accompanied by line references. An LSAT expert knows that content clues almost always refer to something that the author emphasized or about which the author expressed an opinion.

Reading Comp Question Types

Global Question

A question that asks for the Main Idea of the passage or for the author's primary Purpose in writing the passage. Typical question stems:

Which one of the following most accurately expresses the main point of the passage?

The primary purpose of the passage is to

Detail Question

A question that asks what the passage explicitly states about a detail. Typical question stems:

According to the passage, some critics have criticized Gilliam's films on the grounds that

The passage states that one role of a municipality's comptroller in budget decisions by the city council is to

The author identifies which one of the following as a commonly held but false preconception?

The passage contains sufficient information to answer which of the following questions?

Occasionally, the test will ask for a correct answer that contains a detail *not* stated in the passage:

The author attributes each of the following positions to the Federalists EXCEPT:

Inference Question

A question that asks for a statement that follows from or is based on the passage but that is not necessarily stated explicitly in the passage. Some Inference questions contain research clues. The following are typical Inference question stems containing research clues:

Based on the passage, the author would be most likely to agree with which one of the following statements about unified field theory?

The passage suggests which one of the following about the behavior of migratory water fowl?

Given the information in the passage, to which one of the following would radiocarbon dating techniques likely be applicable?

Other Inference questions lack research clues in the question stem. They may be evaluated using the test taker's Big Picture

Summaries, or the answer choices may make it clear that the test taker should research a particular part of the passage text. The following are typical Inference question stems containing research clues:

It can be inferred from the passage that the author would be most likely to agree that

Which one of the following statements is most strongly supported by the passage?

Other Reading Comprehension question types categorized as Inference questions are Author's Attitude questions and Vocabulary-in-Context questions.

Logic Function Question

A question that asks why the author included a particular detail or reference in the passage or how the author used a particular detail or reference. Typical question stems:

The author of the passage mentions declining inner-city populations in the paragraph most likely in order to

The author's discussion of Rimbaud's travels in the Mediterranean (lines 23–28) functions primarily to

Which one of the following best expresses the function of the third paragraph in the passage?

Logic Reasoning Question

A question that asks the test taker to apply Logical Reasoning skills in relation to a Reading Comprehension passage. Logic Reasoning questions often mirror Strengthen or Parallel Reasoning questions, and occasionally mirror Method of Argument or Principle questions. Typical question stems:

Which one of the following, if true, would most strengthen the claim made by the author in the last sentence of the passage (lines 51–55)?

Which one of the following pairs of proposals is most closely analogous to the pair of studies discussed in the passage?

Author's Attitude Question

A question that asks for the author's opinion or point of view on the subject discussed in the passage or on a detail mentioned in the passage. Since the correct answer may follow from the passage without being explicitly stated in it, some Author's Attitude questions are characterized as a subset of Inference questions. Typical question stems:

The author's attitude toward the use of DNA evidence in the appeals by convicted felons is most accurately described as

The author's stance regarding monetarist economic theories can most accurately be described as one of

Vocabulary-in-Context Question

A question that asks how the author uses a word or phrase within the context of the passage. The word or phrase in question is always one with multiple meanings. Since the correct answer follows from its use in the passage, Vocabulary-in-Context questions are characterized as a subset of Inference questions. Typical question stems:

> Which one of the following is closest in meaning to the word "citation" as it used in the second paragraph of the passage (line 18)?

> In context, the word "enlightenment" (line 24) refers to

Wrong Answer Types in RC

Outside the Scope (Out of Scope; Beyond the Scope)

An answer choice containing a statement that is too broad, too narrow, or beyond the purview of the passage

180

An answer choice that directly contradicts what the correct answer must say

Extreme

An answer choice containing language too emphatic (e.g., *all*, *never*, *every*, *none*) to be supported by the passage

Distortion

An answer choice that mentions details or ideas from the passage but mangles or misstates what the author said about those details or ideas

Faulty Use of Detail

An answer choice that accurately states something from the passage but in a manner that incorrectly answers the question

Half-Right/Half-Wrong

An answer choice in which one clause follows from the passage while another clause contradicts or deviates from the passage

Formal Logic Terms

Conditional Statement ("If"-Then Statement)

A statement containing a sufficient clause and a necessary clause. Conditional statements can be described in Formal Logic shorthand as:

> If [sufficient clause] $\rightarrow$ [necessary clause]

In some explanations, the LSAT expert may refer to the sufficient clause as the statement's "trigger" and to the necessary clause as the statement's result.

For more on how to interpret, describe, and use conditional statements on the LSAT, please refer to "A Note About Formal Logic on the LSAT" in this book's introduction.

Contrapositive

The conditional statement logically equivalent to another conditional statement formed by reversing the order of and negating the terms in the original conditional statement. For example, reversing and negating the terms in this statement:

> **If   A $\rightarrow$ B**

results in its contrapositive:

> **If   ~B $\rightarrow$ ~A**

To form the contrapositive of conditional statements in which either the sufficient clause or the necessary clause has more than one term, you must also change the conjunction *and* to *or*, or vice versa. For example, reversing and negating the terms and changing *and* to *or* in this statement:

> **If   M $\rightarrow$ O AND P**

results in its contrapositive:

> **If   ~O OR ~P $\rightarrow$ ~M**

CPSIA information can be obtained
at www.ICGtesting.com
Printed in the USA
LVHW101944291119
638994LV00006B/13/P